THE INGATHERING
OF ISRAEL

THE INGATHERING OF ISRAEL

*A life called to miraculously
help Jewish people return
to their homeland*

Esther Lever

with
Russell Bowles

Sovereign World

Sovereign World Ltd
PO Box 784
Ellel
Lancaster LA1 9DA
England

www.sovereignworld.com
Twitter: @sovereignworld
Facebook: www.facebook.com/sovereignworld

ISBN: 978 1 85240 710 0

The publishers aim to produce books which will help to extend and build up the
Kingdom of God. We do not necessarily agree with every view expressed by the
authors, or with every interpretation of Scripture expressed. We expect readers to
make their own judgment in the light of their understanding of God's Word and
in an attitude of Christian love and fellowship.

Printed in the United Kingdom

Contents

I dedicate this book:

Firstly and most importantly to my Lord and Saviour
Jesus Christ, for without Him I am nothing

To my precious children and grandchildren who had to put
up with my constant absences and travels, often not knowing
where I was and not always understanding what I was doing

To the many, many prayer partners who supported me with
prayer cover, love, and sacrificial giving, enabling me
to go wherever the Lord sent me

To Marilyn Shepherd who has faithfully sent out my
newsletters for over twenty-six years, often at short
notice, and at her own expense

ACKNOWLEDGEMENTS

I wish to express my thanks to the following people whom the Lord sent my way to help me in this project:

To Russell Bowles for offering to shadow write this book. Without his encouragement I doubt it would have been done.

To Peter Barraclough for his capable proofreading.

To the Ebenezer "family" for their constant, faithful work in which I have been privileged to participate.

To Ellel Ministries for their teaching and loving ministry which set me free, enabling me to be bold in my faith to serve the Lord in His calling.

To my friend Hannah (not her real name) who taught me so much, and the many people who gave me hospitality wherever I went.

Lastly, to dear Ann and Bill who allowed me to use their home as a base when the Lord called me to sell mine and be a "tramp" for Him.

FOREWORD

Why should you read this book? I think it is worth reading for several reasons but not least because it's about the remarkable things God has done in the ministry of Esther Lever.

I would hazard a guess that all those who have prayed for and supported her while she has been travelling the world in search of Jewish communities would say that Esther is pretty remarkable herself. I certainly think she is for her willingness to put up with danger, discomfort, and problems at an age when most of us are looking to put our feet up and take it easy.

She has a determination to be obedient to her Lord, and because of this God has been able to use her as a support to Jewish people in many remote parts of the earth.

To enable her to fulfil her calling, God has intervened many times in supernatural ways and sometimes by angelic visitations. The stories of the people and events she describes make inspirational reading.

It has been my privilege to know Esther for some years now. I know her motive for writing this book is not to attract attention to herself. It is rather to respond to God's prompting to write it in order to show that He has in no way cast aside the Jewish people but on the contrary has much yet to fulfil in His purposes for them.

As Esther sought to obey God's call on her life, she always insisted that the vision for the work came from Him, the day-by-day instructions came from Him, and the results came from Him. Therefore to no one else but Him is the glory due. What you will read in these pages brings glory to the God of Israel and reveals that His heart for His people has never changed despite what some may say.

If you have an interest at all in Israel and the Jewish people, you will enjoy this book. If you are new to this subject or think that the Church has replaced Israel in God's plans, let me briefly explain.

The State of Israel came into being in 1948 for no other reason than that it was God's will. Yes, the catalyst was the Holocaust when six million Jewish people lost their lives in the gas chambers of Nazi Germany, causing the world to realize that they needed a homeland; but in essence it came about simply because it was the will of Almighty God. The prophet Isaiah says:

> *Who has heard such a thing? Who has seen such things?*
> *Can a land be born in one day?*
> *Can a nation be brought forth all at once?*
>
> (Isaiah 66:8)

That day was 14 May 1948.

If you are a Christian believer in the God of Israel and have read your Bible with open eyes, you will realize that the eternal purposes of God for the Jewish people are not finished. In fact their destiny is intertwined with the future of that tract of land that the Romans named Palestine, which God promised Abram centuries before through the covenant He made with him in Genesis 15. Why else would God say in forty-seven places in the Bible that He promised this land to the Jews?

No other nation on earth has been promised a piece of land by God – not even the British who had the greatest empire this world has ever seen. Therefore we know that the Jews were singled out for divine purposes. These purposes were firstly to be a people for God's own possession who would be an example to the nations in order to show forth His ways; and secondly to bring forth the Messiah through whom the whole world could receive salvation.

That the Jews failed in the first of these great purposes did not prevent them from succeeding in the second: bringing forth the Way of Salvation, Jesus – or Yeshua as He is called in Hebrew, a name which actually means "salvation" in that language. In fact their rejection of Him as Messiah was the catalyst that caused the gospel to be preached to all peoples. Just think: if the Jews had accepted Jesus, they would not have allowed Him to be crucified and the apostles would not have gone far and wide, preaching to the Gentiles! It was the Jews' rejection of Him that caused salvation to come to the whole world. As St Paul says:

> By their transgression salvation has come to the Gentiles . . .
>
> (Romans 11:11b)

Today there is much demonizing of the State of Israel within Christian circles, much of it by senior members of the clergy who ought to know better, and all because they look at the issue through political rather than Biblical eyes. The rebirth of the modern State after approximately 2,000 years is nothing less than God fulfilling His promises. Would you expect anything less of God?

You may say, "But the Jews were disobedient in what God called them to."

You are right. God put before them obedience and disobedience: one brought reward; the other brought judgement in increasing measure until at last they were expelled from the land God had given them. He warned them that this would happen.

"There you are then!" you exclaim. "They were out and God has finished with them."

But hold on there; look more closely at the covenant God made with their father Abraham – or Abram as he then was. It was the custom in the ancient world, when making a covenant, that pieces of heifer, goat, ram, and birds were laid out and the two parties to the covenant walked between the pieces. In Genesis 15 we read that when God made this covenant, Abram fell into a deep sleep and God alone walked between the pieces. Because Abram was asleep He was not an active participant in the process and therefore only God was covenanted to keep what was decreed. Therefore the promise of the land to Abram and his descendants was in no way conditional on their being willing to keep to anything. It was simply a promise that God made.

However, even though the *promise* of the Land of Israel to the Jews wasn't conditional, their *occupation* of it was, and this was why, when they transgressed, God had to keep His Word and eventually expel them. But He always included the promise of restoration – the land was always theirs to come back to; it didn't belong to anyone else. In Psalm 105:10–11 we are told that God had given it to the Jews "as an everlasting covenant." "Everlasting" means exactly what it says. This was why, during the Babylonian exile, Jeremiah was able under God's prompting to say that it would last seventy years and then there would be restoration. God keeps His promises. The expulsion was the responsibility of the Jewish nation; their restoration was a promise of God.

That God should give His Word and later break it is as unthinkable as the sun not rising in the morning or the waves not roaring in the sea. His righteous character makes it impossible for Him to break His Word. He is not like man who breaks covenants as it suits him. As it says in the book of Numbers:

> *God is not a man, that He should lie,*
> *Nor a son of man, that He should repent;*
> *Has He said, and will He not do it?*
> *Or has He spoken, and will He not make it good?*

(Numbers 23:19)

To say that God has finished with His purposes for the Jews or that the Land of Israel doesn't belong to them is to deny His righteous character and call Him a covenant breaker. It is very serious.

The prophet Ezekiel declared that it was not for the Jews' sake that the Lord would gather them back to their land but rather because it was a matter of the honor of His Holy Name (Ezekiel 36:22–24). God's character had been profaned among the nations and He had to do something about it. If He didn't act to bring the Jews back to their land, He would be seen as a covenant breaker in the eyes of the world.

If God were to break His promises to the Jews, could you be sure that He wouldn't break His promises to you? For no other reason do we know we can trust Him than that His character is flawless. He therefore has to bring the Jews back to the land that He promised them.

Part of God's ingathering of the Jews to the Land is His desire that they should have a final chance to recognize the One who is their Messiah. It is Jesus alone who, at the end of an unprecedented period of Jewish persecution called the Great Tribulation, will gather all the remaining Jews from around the world back to Israel when He returns to the earth to reign during the millennium. What an amazing event that will be! What we are seeing now is merely a trickle.

In Romans 11:15 St Paul affirms that when the Jews finally recognize their Messiah it will be like life from the dead!

So you see, those who look upon the Jews as a people rejected by God are in effect calling Him a liar. But He is holy and utterly reliable: He will keep His Word. He promised and He will fulfil - it is as simple and profound as that.

Read on – you will enjoy what lies within these pages. And may the God of Israel and the Jewish Messiah, Jesus, open your eyes to His eternal purposes.

Russell Bowles

Thus says the LORD,
Who gives the sun for light by day
And the fixed order of the moon and the stars for light by night,
Who stirs up the sea so that its waves roar;
The LORD of hosts is His name:
"If this fixed order departs
From before Me," declares the LORD,
"Then the offspring of Israel also will cease
From being a nation before Me forever."

(Jeremiah 31:35–36)

PREFACE

You did not choose Me but I chose you, and appointed you that you
would go and bear fruit.

(John 15:16a)

God is very gracious. He took me, someone who is nothing special,
and has used me. He will use you too if you will allow Him
access to the depths of your heart. I was broken when I cried out to
God to give me something to do. He looks for those who are broken
before Him and who are willing to obey. He doesn't look for the strong
or the brilliant, for the powerful or the wealthy. He looks for the
ordinary person who is willing to put their plans and ideas aside and
run with God's plans and ideas. That's all He wants.

He never gives us things to do that are beyond our capabilities, but
He often trains us to do things which we didn't think we were capable
of. It has seemed to me that often this training was happening when I
didn't realize it. Indeed I am convinced that what we are doing today is
a preparation for what God has for us to do tomorrow.

God uses all sorts of situations too. When I was volunteering in
Israel, working with children who had severe learning difficulties and
physical challenges, I learned a great deal. Some of these children had

the mental age of babies and would be sick over me. I would clean it up and it would happen again. I learned patience!

When I worked in a hospital with the chronically ill, I helped to feed patients who dribbled all over their clothes. I learned compassion! It was all training for the things I was to face later in my calling.

I wouldn't pretend for one minute that God's training isn't difficult. It certainly can be, but the wonderful thing is that while He is training us He is gently changing us to be more and more like Jesus. I have met people like that – people who shine with a beautiful radiance and have an aura of deep peace – and I long to be like them.

Part of my training was involvement with Ellel Ministries, a non-denominational organization that specializes in spiritual, emotional, and physical healing. It is surprising how many of us struggle with issues in our personalities that are there because of wounds in the past. Gentle ministry can enable people to become more whole. Part of this is healing the broken-hearted and preaching deliverance to the captives, which is an aim taken from Isaiah 61.

My first visit to this organization involved taking a group of people for their benefit, but God spoke to me that I needed ministry too. I had been a middle child, striving for attention, working hard, needing to be noticed. I had a lot of pain hidden away that needed the touch of God. It was wonderful to be released from it.

Since that first visit, I felt led to participate in several of the courses and teaching seminars. I have also become an associate prayer minister so I too can bring help to others, though of course I am still a work in progress myself!

In my calling I am completely dependent on the Lord leading me, either into situations or out of them, and am often asked, "How do you hear from God?" This is a natural question. Jesus said, "My sheep hear My voice" (John 10:27a). We can therefore be certain that it is His will that we hear Him. But why do so many of us find this a troublesome subject? I had the same question when I had cancer and decided I would seek God until I got the answer.

Jeremiah 29:13 says:

> You will seek Me and find Me when you search for Me with all
> your heart.

During my days of searching, some of my friends brought me books
to read about people who had had miracles happen in their lives. As I
read, something struck me quite forcibly: these people talked to God
as if they were talking with someone in the same room. And they got
answers! I wanted to be like them and I cried out to God to do the
same thing for me.

I cannot say the results happened immediately. Rather it was a
process like the dawn light that creeps over a hill in the morning,
gradually extending its influence into every area.

I noticed that sometimes, when I was reading the Bible, verses
would impress themselves on me, or the text seemed to stand out. At
other times a verse would leap from the page with its message.

Then I found that I would get a distinct feeling that I should go
somewhere or do something.

It was only later that I began to receive "words," that is, thoughts
that would come unbidden – what the Bible calls a "still small voice"
(1 Kings 19:12 KJV). And very occasionally it would be the audible voice
of God.

Today it can be in any of these ways that the Lord speaks to me.

We are all individuals, and God treats us as such and with respect.
He won't force Himself into our lives but if we take steps towards Him,
He will hold His arms out to receive us. He is willing to use us but,
more importantly, He desires to change us. Without our being willing
to be changed, there is no way He can use us. All He desires is a willing
heart. Let's be willing!

So much of my calling – the greater part, in fact – has been as
an instrument of comfort and help to the Jewish people. God has
laid on my heart His own feelings for them, allowing me to feel

some of His pain when they have been mistreated and some of His joy at their restoration to the land that He promised them so many millennia ago. This joy is rooted in the fact that His divine purposes are coming together in preparation for the return of the Messiah. The ingathering of the Jewish people to their ancient homeland is part of that preparation.

It has been my privilege to travel to many parts of the world in the fulfilment of my calling, and I have seen God do amazing and miraculous things without which I would not have been able to complete any of the tasks He gave me.

In writing this book I have desired to show that God can take and use anybody if they are willing, but more importantly that it is God Himself who puts plans together and God Himself who completes and accomplishes everything. If it had been left to me, nothing would have been achieved! For this reason then, I have published this book in the hope that people will see that it is God who is behind the ingathering of the Jewish people. He will do it with or without us, because it is for the glory of His Holy Name.

Esther Lever
Monks Risborough
2012

Therefore say to the house of Israel, "Thus says the Lord GOD, 'It is not for your sake, O house of Israel, that I am about to act, but for My holy name . . .'"

(Ezekiel 36:22a)

CHAPTER I

HOW THE LORD CALLED ME

I will instruct you and teach you in the way which you should go;
I will counsel you with My eye upon you.

(Psalm 32:8)

I saw the ambulance as we turned into our road. With my heart feeling as if it was coming out of my chest I accelerated hard and pulled up at our house. Jumping out, I raced up the path, but a man in uniform wouldn't let me in. My daughter sped past us both and went inside. I looked at the man's ashen face, and his next words caused me to collapse into his arms.

He said, "I'm afraid I have some sad news, madam. Your husband has passed away."

It was 1982 and I was almost fifty.

The days passed slowly and painfully, stretching into long weeks of emptiness. I sat around the house a lot. Family and friends offered comfort, but my heart ached and I began to cry out to God.

"Give me something to do," I prayed. "Please give me something to do!"

He must have heard me, for the very next day a friend from church called round with a book saying, "You ought to read this – it's really interesting."

The book was *Appointment in Jerusalem*, by Derek Prince, and told the story of his first wife's call to live in that city and rescue Jewish and Arab children.

I spent the next few days engrossed in the book, captivated by this Danish woman who gave up a comfortable life to live in less than comfortable surroundings. She took in one or two children who needed care, and this number soon grew. It wasn't long before she had several children, both Jewish and Arab, who looked to her as their adopted mother.

A strange feeling began to stir in my heart as I read the descriptions of the Old City and its residents. I began to feel a desire to go there, and said to my youngest daughter, "I believe the Lord may be calling me to go to Jerusalem."

"Don't be silly, Mum," was her response. "It's just your imagination. Put that book away." However, I felt a seed had been planted in my heart and I carried on reading.

Over the next few days and weeks, I mused on this unexpected desire to go to Jerusalem.

It seems a strange place to send me, I thought, as I was considering it one day, *but I'm glad it's not the Soviet Union*. In those days news was rife about the persecution of Christians in the communist world. Labour camps and torture were not things I wanted to face! *No, Israel is better. After all, Jesus was Jewish so it must be fairly easy to tell His people about Him.*

How much I had to learn! I knew nothing of the anti-Semitism in the Church or of the terrible ways Christians had mistreated Jews down the centuries – nothing even about the Holocaust. I had been a child during the Second World War but my parents had shielded me from the terrible news that had come out of Germany as I was not allowed to read the newspapers.

As I thought about this call that seemed to have taken root in my soul, I decided to talk to my pastor and also to the city missioner, whose job it was to spread the gospel in the local area. My pastor was quite positive and thought the Lord might indeed be speaking to me. The city missioner, on the other hand, was dismissive and said there was plenty to do locally.

About this time, a friend came to see me with a brochure for tours to Israel. I thought, *I wonder if this is what the Lord had in mind – just a holiday.* I'd had a recent tax rebate so the money was there if I needed it. My friend, who was unemployed, said she would go with me if she managed to secure a job. So we put a "fleece" before the Lord and prayed that if it was right for us to go on this trip, she would get a job. Two days later she had three interviews and was offered one of the positions. We booked the tour for August.

It was very hot in Israel when we arrived – we had completely overlooked the summer temperatures! I loved the countryside: the beautiful citrus groves, pines, and olive trees. Some of these olives were many hundreds of years old, witnesses to a varied and violent history. There were a few still standing in the Garden of Gethsemane that were thought to date back 2,000 years and might have seen the Lord Jesus walk among them. It was awe-inspiring.

We had a superb guide who took us to all the famous places and I kept close to him at each site, not wanting to miss a word. In addition he explained the modern history of his country, which by then had been established for only thirty-five years.

Somehow the Land had an impact on me in a way I had never expected. I fell in love with it, weeping at the slightest thing, especially whenever I saw elderly Jews.

We finished the tour in Netanya, and on our last evening the guide unexpectedly asked me to take a walk with him along the cliff tops. We got into a discussion about religion so I started to tell him about Jesus. However, talking of the cross produced an angry reaction in him and he began to shout: "Who is this man Jesus? So he died on a cross! Thousands died on crosses."

Back at the hotel my roommate was already sound asleep so I undressed quietly and got into bed. Sometime in the night I woke up. I was wide awake and aware that the silence seemed to have a feeling of expectancy. Into my head came the story of Samuel who heard the Lord's voice in the temple. Folding my arms across my chest and feeling a bit self-conscious, I said, "Speak, Lord. Your servant is listening."

Immediately, and seemingly from all around the ceiling, came several voices all saying the same thing. It was the phrase used by the guide on the cliff tops: "Who is this man Jesus?" The voices repeated this question over and over.

Then I heard the Lord Himself say in a heartbroken voice, "My own people – they don't know me."

I began to cry and cry but couldn't understand why.

I got up, went into the bathroom, and knelt down, asking the Lord what to do. A vision came to me – a beautiful picture of an arch made of cream Jerusalem stone with a path through it and a blue sky above. The Lord spoke to me and said, "Follow the path and read Isaiah 55."

The next morning I read the passage and saw instantly how it fitted my life and seemed to be calling me to serve the Lord. We had a pastor on the tour with us so I found him and told him what had happened. He listened carefully and then read me two portions of Scripture from Zechariah chapter 8:

> I will return to Zion and will dwell in the midst of Jerusalem.
>
> (verse 3a)

> Behold, I am going to save My people from the land of the east and from the land of the west; and I will bring them back.
>
> (verses 7–8a)

The pastor said that he believed God was indeed calling me to

Jerusalem. I was so thrilled and excited that I could have stayed in Israel and not returned home! However, very wisely he told me not to rush into anything but to go back to England to await further instructions from the Lord.

People on the tour had told me of two organizations: Prayer for Israel and the International Christian Embassy Jerusalem (ICEJ). These had offices in England and when I returned home I wrote to both, telling them of the call I'd had. To my disappointment, both wrote back saying that everyone who goes to Israel thinks they should return. They also suggested there were ways to support the Jewish people in England, for example through local prayer groups. So I joined one nearby and made some good friends. Something, however, kept nagging at me inside. I couldn't shake the feeling that I should be in Israel, so I cried out to God again, asking Him to make His will known to Me.

I said to the Lord, "Please, Lord; I need someone in the Land to say 'Come.'"

While waiting for replies to my letters, I had sought out and got to know the local Jewish community. There was something very special about them and I found myself attending *Shabbat* (Sabbath) services at their synagogue most Saturdays. I loved it.

I was continuing to seek God for confirmation of His calling and I asked Him to get me Hebrew lessons on a one-to-one basis if He was really sending me to Israel. I thought this would be really difficult for Him.

I attended the synagogue one Saturday, and on this occasion the service was being led by a different man, not the usual leader. His Hebrew was fluent and when I commented on this afterwards, he said he was a Hebrew teacher. I started to get excited but my enthusiasm was short-lived as he couldn't help me at that time. He did, however, give me an address to send away for a textbook. When it came and I looked at it, I realized I was going to have trouble with the pronunciation of this language. I took it back to the synagogue and showed it to the

President, Mr Weintraub. He suggested that I come to his home where he would help me. It wasn't until three weeks later that I realized I was having Hebrew lessons one to one. God had done it! I was beginning to understand that He was God of the impossible.

About this time, I was given a specific Scripture verse as confirmation of my call:

> I am sending you to the people of Israel.
>
> (Ezekiel 2:3 NIrV)

I have found, many times in my walk with God, that when He is in some idea or plan He makes sure it happens. He only needs us to be willing and available. I was – very much so!

A short time later I received a reply from the Jerusalem office of the International Christian Embassy. It said, "Come out for an extended time and see if the Lord opens a door for you."

Here was the answer I had prayed for. I was so happy! This was October 1983. As a result of all these confirmations, I contacted the lady who had written to me and arranged to go to Jerusalem for six weeks.

Before I left, two important things happened. First, my friends at the Prayer for Israel group said I ought to meet a Swiss businessman, Gustav Scheller, who lived in Bournemouth. Secondly, I received an invitation to visit the pastor who had been with me on my tour to Israel.

In Bournemouth, Gustav and his wife Elsa were organizing meetings of a group called Let My People Go. Its members met monthly to pray and discuss topics related to helping the Jewish people get out of communist countries where they were persecuted. This group was about to host a speaker called Steve Lightle who had had a vision of thousands of Jews coming out of Russia. He had also published a book, *Exodus II*, which gave the details of the vision.

I went to the meeting. The huge centre was packed with enthusiastic supporters, some of whom decided they should make preparations for any Jews who might need accommodation on their "exodus." I found it all fascinating, not realizing its significance or how important my contact with Gustav Scheller was to become in the years ahead.

I then went to see the pastor who had counselled me on my Israel tour. His family lived in the north of England and, while there, I visited the church where he had grown up. A member of the congregation unnerved me by saying that I would be preaching that Sunday!

"Oh no, I don't preach," I said. "You've got it all wrong."

The man was very insistent, however, so I sought the Lord that evening. Surprisingly, I began to feel that this was indeed His will. I had never preached before. What would I speak about? I felt impressed to get a notepad and pen. While I prayed, certain numbers came into my head so I wrote them down. Then came a Scripture verse:

You shall be holy, for I am holy.

(1 Peter 1:16)

I found myself writing some notes on holy living and what it means for our modern lifestyle. It turned out that the numbers I'd received were those of hymns which fitted the theme of holiness. I was nervous about preaching but it was obviously the Lord's will.

The day of the service arrived. I preached, and amazingly a young woman committed her life to Jesus. I was really excited! The Lord was really stretching me and I knew it was all part of His plan for the next phase of my life.

I returned home and made final preparations for my extended visit to Israel. It was September 1984.

I arrived in Jerusalem just before *Succot* or "the Feast of Tabernacles" as we say in English. The ICEJ held their own version of this feast to which hundreds of people came from around the world. It was all very new to me but I loved every minute. The sights and sounds of Jerusalem proved a heady mix which captivated and enthralled me. However, I was really there to see what God wanted me to do.

I was given a list of Jewish organizations in need of volunteers and started to visit each one of them in turn, asking the Lord to get me invited if one of these was His place for me. The last one was a home for children with severe mental and physical disabilities.

I went along and visited the children. The poor little things lay on mats outside, benefitting from the fresh air but disturbed by flies landing on their faces. Their carers seemed to spend all their time shooing away the flies! I was a little dubious about what use I would be, but it was suggested that I help out for three days to see how I got on. I prayed, "Please, Lord, if it is Your will for me to work here, give me a love for these children."

I arrived the next morning and went inside, where an array of cots faced me. One child was crying, and as I went over and reached out to offer some comfort, a great love flowed down my arms to him. God had done it! I picked up the little child and loved him, later finding that I felt this way about all the children who came into my care.

I was invited to work there as a volunteer and so started full-time at this home in December 1984. One might ask what this work had to do with my later call to assist Jews in different parts of the world. I believe God used my time at the children's home to teach me many things about myself, about His grace and mercy, and how to depend on Him for everything I needed. I was there for almost sixteen months with two breaks away for visa renewal.

While in Jerusalem, I came into contact again with Gustav Scheller, the man who had organized the meeting for Steve Lightle in Bournemouth. He put on a prayer conference in Jerusalem each January and I became involved, coming to know him quite well and realizing that God's hand was upon him in a remarkable way. I kept in touch with him and also with Ebenezer Operation Exodus, the organization he founded later on to assist Jewish people to go to Israel.

It was part way through 1985 and I had been in Israel for eight months. I was walking along a street in Jerusalem when I heard a voice say, "Why have you got a house?"

Startled, I looked round, but there was nobody there. "Is that You, Lord?" I asked.

The Lord spoke to me in an audible voice about my house, saying that I did not need it. I pondered on this conversation for some time, wondering if I should sell the house or rent it out.

I went back to England to renew my visa and as I walked through the door the phone rang. It was a friend saying she had a message for me: she thought the Lord wanted me to sell my house! She gave me the following Scripture:

> You must leave the city to camp in the open field.
>
> (Micah 4:10 NIV)

I was amazed, but knew then that God did indeed want me to put my home up for sale.

And so the house was sold, the money shared between my children (now all grown up), and the contents given away. The Lord had somebody in mind for every item – a story in itself – and it all took only a month.

What a blessing it proved to be! I was free to go wherever God wanted me to go with no worries about a house in England. It was quite liberating and God always looked after me. I was without a home for nearly twelve years and yet I always had a bed for the night – sometimes in some strange places but God always provided. I made a deal with God that if I ever had to ask anyone for a bed for the night I would consider He had let me down. I never had to ask; I was invited to stay somewhere every night. It was a blessed time.

While I was in England, Kevin, the pastor friend from my Israel tour, invited me to his church in North Wales. He and I found that the Lord was building a special unity in the Holy Spirit between us. The Lord would often tell us the same things, which led to some special trips together to pray in particular places.

Around Easter time I went up to North Wales and Kevin made me welcome. The next morning he said, "We have to go out somewhere today, don't we?"

"Yes," I replied. "The Lord told me we need to go to the mountains."

"Well, you navigate then," he suggested with a smile.

After breakfast we got into his car and set off in the general direction of the mountains. I concentrated on listening to the Lord, and it was as if Someone touched my arms if we were to go left or right. At other times I became aware of a picture in my mind: a line curling away to the right or left, indicating the direction.

When we got near the hills around Mt Snowdon, I felt we should pull over into a lay-by ahead. We then walked up to a nearby knoll with a wonderful view of the valley below, lit up by the sunshine. At this time Steve Lightle (the man I'd heard in Bournemouth) was on a prayer journey through Russia. He and some others were praying in different places, asking God to release the Jews to go back to Israel. As we stood on this knoll, Kevin and I felt led by the Holy Spirit to pray for Steve's team.

The Lord then spoke to me, telling me to look down the valley at a cottage and a flock of sheep bathed in beautiful sunshine. He then said, "Look up." I saw the top of Snowdon shrouded in mist and looking very cold.

"I'm giving you a choice," He said. "You may go the way of the valley and I will be glorified. But if you go the way of the mountaintop, alone, in high and dangerous places, I will be glorified even more. You may choose."

I realized that to "go the way of the valley" meant I could probably marry again and serve God somewhere safe and comfortable. I thought for a few seconds. How could I choose that way if God could be more glorified another way? No, I would choose the mountaintop.

The next time I was there in North Wales, Kevin and I both knew we must go to Liverpool. Again I was to navigate, but I had never been to Liverpool before and had no idea of the direction. Therefore once more I had to rely on listening for the gentle nudging and impressions of the Holy Spirit to direct us. To this day I don't know the route we took, but we got to Liverpool and felt we should go to the Anglican cathedral. Questions ran through my mind as we walked up the steps. Would we meet someone inside? Would someone need prayer or help?

We went through the large door and turned a corner, where I was stopped in my tracks. There was a huge wooden cross with a white cloth draped diagonally over one beam. I was transfixed for a moment and felt impressed to sit on a nearby pew. I gazed at the cross.

Suddenly I became aware that the Lord Himself was right beside me. My eyes were closed and I felt I dared not open them, for I knew He was there. He spoke to me about what had happened in the Garden of Gethsemane the night before His crucifixion. He had been faced with a decision – to choose the cross or not. In my spirit I knew He was holding out to me one of the rough-hewn nails with which He had been fixed to the cross. It was about 18 centimetres long and tapered to a roughly made point.

He said, "I am giving *you* a choice. You may choose to share with Me in My suffering and I will be more glorified. You choose."

I didn't stop to think. I just nodded and said, "Yes, if You will be more glorified."

And then He was gone.

How could anyone say "No"? I thought.

In another corner of this great cathedral was a model of the empty tomb. I felt I should sit down and look at it. Again I felt the Lord draw near; He was so close. He whispered in my ear, "Would you die for Me so that I would be more glorified?"

Again I said, "Yes, Lord." I really felt I would not mind dying for Him.

And once again He was gone.

We made our way back to North Wales. I felt overwhelmed by all that had happened and made preparations for my return to the children's home in Jerusalem.

Back in Israel I began to think about what I had said to the Lord and the whole idea of suffering. I started to feel uneasy about it. If I were in prison and tortured, how would I cope? What if I were branded with hot irons or had my nails pulled out? I had heard of such things happening. I didn't mind the idea of dying; but suffering . . . that was something else. I shared my concerns with some friends, fearing that in a difficult situation I might let the Lord down.

Some months later I had to go back to England, and once more Kevin asked me to share in his church about what I was doing in Israel. Early one morning the Lord spoke to both of us separately and said we were to go to Manchester. Kevin had been there only once and said again that I should navigate. As before, I had to pay careful attention to the guidance of the Holy Spirit: the "hand" lightly brushing my arms for left or right; or the "line" in my mind showing the route we had to follow.

When we reached the city, neither Kevin nor I had any idea where we were exactly, or even what we were looking for. Around us were the suburbs of a sprawling metropolis – that's all we knew. We kept driving and crossed a junction, and suddenly we both knew we had gone too far.

"Stop and turn around," I said. "This isn't right."

Kevin agreed and swung the car round. Immediately into view came a large building, and on its wall was a figure of Jesus on the cross.

"That's it!" I cried, knowing we had found our goal. But Kevin had already discerned this.

We parked the car, walked to the building, and went through a large gate onto a gravelled drive. We were walking purposefully as if we knew what we were doing. It seemed that Someone else was in charge of my legs as I strode out in front, leading the way. I turned right, following a path between buildings. No one saw us. Then we passed through a small white gate into a garden; there was a tree stump on the lawn and I knew I should go and sit on it. However, as it was winter, thick frost covered the lawn and I felt reluctant to trample the grass.

"Go on," said Kevin. "You have to sit on that stump."

It was amazing how we could both sense what the Holy Spirit wanted. So I went across the lawn and sat down, finding myself facing the wall with the figure of Jesus on the cross.

Into my head came the thought: *Jesus is not on the cross.* Suddenly it seemed as if the cross released Him, and He came down. He was right there beside me, sitting with me in that garden, but as if we were in a bubble. The Lord was wearing a pale blue robe and our heads were bowed towards each other, close but not touching.

"I have heard what you have been saying about suffering," Jesus said. "I want to talk to you about it and I want you to choose again."

He went on to tell me that my future would not be as I had feared. It would be quite different and nothing I couldn't cope with. He would not give me anything I was not able to bear and He would always be with me. He assured me that there were different forms of suffering, and He said I should think carefully and not hurry my answer. But I already knew what it was going to be. The Lord was so reassuring that I said again, "Yes."

He talked to me a little more about His calling on my life and told me He had plans and purposes for me, but He didn't say what they were.

Then suddenly He was gone and I found myself sitting all alone. I looked up – and the figure of Jesus was there on the wall.

Had I imagined all that had happened? Future events proved that I hadn't.

Back in Israel the next Sunday, I asked the Lord what I should do that day. He told me to go to Yad Vashem, the Israeli Holocaust memorial.

"But Lord," I protested, "I've been there four times already."

"Go again," was all He said. So I did.

This time I felt I should walk through the grounds around the main buildings, where I had never been before. There were separate areas, each with a memorial for a town or a village where atrocities had taken place, even for a group of individuals or a family. As I went, a pain grew in my heart for all the evil that had been done against this people. Then suddenly I saw it: a sculptured figure of a woman in a long robe. She had a huge pile of stones at her feet and she was covering her face in grief. These stones represented the children that had been murdered.

I was filled with an indescribable pain. I was distraught. I heard the Lord asking me to get a stone and put it there for *Him*. I did this silently, weeping, overcome with grief. I felt that the pain was His pain. Later on I sat on a nearby wall, feeling as if I had been wrung out like a wet rag. I said to the Lord, "What is it all about, Lord?"

In a broken voice He replied, "You are sharing in My suffering – just a little."

Then I understood. If that was only a little part, how great must His suffering be for everything that had happened to His people in the Holocaust!

Many times in later years I stood in places where there had been atrocities. Pains akin to arthritis would shoot up my legs. This happened at Babi Yar in Kiev where thousands of Jewish men, women, and children had been shot over the course of a few days and thrown into pits. I had the same sensation at Ponary in Lithuania where there is a mass grave and also at Tiananmen Square in Beijing where students were massacred. The Lord feels great pain at the things people do to one another.

During my time at the children's home a strange thing happened. While I was seeking the Lord one day, a line appeared in front of my eyes, on which were two dots: one was Berlin, and the other was Moscow. Was the Lord pointing out a journey I had to make? This seemed clear, but what about the time of the journey? I didn't feel I should go on this trip straight away but knew that very likely I would in the near future. I knew that having a vision was one thing, but it was also crucial to get the time right. Otherwise what the Lord had planned wouldn't be accomplished. I stored this picture away in my heart and awaited further instructions.

I was grateful to the Lord for all He showed me in this training period. He taught me to listen and follow instructions from the Holy Spirit; He allowed me to understand what He meant by sharing in His suffering; and He let me know how to rely upon Him for everything I needed. This proved crucial for the ministry He would eventually lead me into.

After leaving the children's home I spent some time back in the UK with my family, seeking the Lord about His plan for me when I returned to Israel. I had asked Him many times to put me with Jewish people so that I could get more understanding of their way of life.

A little while after I returned to Jerusalem, I was sitting under a tree in the grounds of the Baptist church when a young woman in a pink jacket walked in front of me. As she wandered around the garden it seemed she was often walking past me, and so we eventually smiled at each other and struck up a conversation. It turned out she had to return home to Sweden and needed somebody to look after an old lady. I sensed immediately that God wanted me to volunteer for this task.

The job involved overnight care for an eighty-nine-year-old German Jewish lady who had escaped from the Nazis in 1939. I would need to be in during the evening to put her to bed and on hand during the night in case she needed somebody. I would prepare her breakfast in the morning, when someone else would arrive to take over the day shift. For this I would get a room to stay in, plus my breakfast, and be free throughout the day. It was wonderful.

I was with this lady for a year, during which time I did some volunteer work at Sha'are Zedek hospital. I also took an intensive course in Hebrew at the university on Mt Scopus. Who would have thought that I would be studying Hebrew at a university in Jerusalem in my fifties! God has such amazing plans when we choose to walk with Him.

During this year I learned a great deal about Jewish life; for example, keeping the Sabbath, when a great peace descends on Jerusalem as the shops close and the traffic stops; and about the other feasts. What is more, I learned about the great care the people have for one another.

Early in March 1987 I was in England again for visa renewal when once more God sent me to visit Kevin in North Wales. Again we were directed by the Holy Spirit to go out in the car and again I had to navigate, not knowing the way. We were sent this time to Chester.

On the outskirts of the city we parked the car and walked in towards the shopping area. We both felt we should stop for coffee at an old Anglican church – now a visitor's centre. All the pews were missing except for two rows at the front, and I had the urge to sit there and look at the stained-glass windows. The Lord seemed to speak to me through each design, but at the last one – Jesus' ascension into heaven – He said to me, "I am giving you a new name."

Kevin came and sat next to me. "God is giving you a new name," he said. If he hadn't confirmed this strange message, I might have thought I'd imagined it!

My name was Vera and I wondered what other name I was to be called by. I pondered on different names such as Rachel and Rebecca, but the Lord said to me softly, "I am calling you 'Esther.' You are to be My Esther."

Kevin always seemed to be in tune with what God was saying to me. He opened his Bible at the book of Esther and repeated God's words that I should be called "Esther." He then read to me words from the book exactly as they were being spoken into my heart by the Lord: "For you have been raised up for such a time as this" (see Esther 4:14).

Needless to say, I was rather overcome. The Lord then said, "I am aligning you with My Jewish people."

I then knew I was to read Ruth's words of commitment to Naomi (Ruth 1:16–17) but adapted for myself: "Where they go I will go. Where they dwell I will dwell. Their people shall be my people, their God my God. Where they die I will die and there will I be buried."

This experience was quite awesome. I accepted it deep in my heart but decided to tell no one.

Back in Israel one *Shabbat*, the family of the old lady I looked after came to celebrate with her as they did each week. I was alone in my room praying, kneeling by my bed, when the Lord said to me, "I have called you 'Esther.'"

"Yes," I responded.

He then said gently, "I want you to use it. You are just being proud."

It then dawned on me that I hadn't wanted to tell people my new name because I thought they would laugh at me. I lay face down and confessed the sin of pride. I then went straight out of my room and told all the family members there. They were delighted and completely accepted it, calling me "Esther" from then on.

From that day forward I used this name, at first "Esther-Vera" to help people get used to it, and later on just "Esther." For twenty-five years now I have been known as "Esther," changing my documents to avoid confusion. Like Esther in the Bible, I know I have been raised up for this time. What an amazing God we serve!

It was at *Pesach* (Passover) later in April that my dear old lady died. I had been caring for her each night for a whole year. The Lord in His mercy had now taken her home and that she was with her Messiah I had no doubt. For the first time, I experienced a Jewish funeral and the custom of "keeping *Shiva*," a week of mourning. It was all very special to me.

After this it was time to return to the UK as my visa had expired. As I did so, I wondered, *What next, Lord?*

CHAPTER 2

THE LORD HAD
THE PLAN

"For I know the plans that I have for you," declares the LORD, "plans for welfare and not for calamity to give you a future and a hope."

(Jeremiah 29:11)

I t was *Pesach* 1987 and I had been in Israel for some time, busy with various projects. Now released from my work of caring for the dear old lady, I was open to the Lord showing me what He wanted me to do next. After a time of prayer it seemed clear I was to go back to England. First, however, I felt impressed to travel around Israel and pray at her borders. I also felt moved to climb Mt Sinai before sunrise one morning. It was a rich experience, watching the sun come up, dusting the mountaintops with gold and reflecting in some small measure the glory of God's handiwork. Excitement crept into my heart. I was sure the Lord had something else for me to do!

Back in England, I sought the Lord for direction and recalled a strange experience that I'd had two years previously in May 1985. A line had appeared in front of my eyes, on which were two dots: one was Berlin, and the other was Moscow. It had seemed obvious at the time that this was a journey God wanted me to make. However, I knew that having a vision was one matter, but getting the timing right could be another, and this was crucial to success.

As I was praying for direction, I remembered this vision and felt the Lord confirm the timing. This journey was not a small matter. I had never done anything like it before. I was alone, knew nothing about communism, and didn't speak either German or Russian. God would have to do everything if I was going to undertake this trip.

I soon learned that if God wants something done He puts the right people in your path, creates the right opportunities, and sets things up for you. In the spring of the previous year, at a meeting of an organization called Prayer for Israel in London, I had met a Polish lady. She was talking about building a house on a farm – before the very eyes of the communists – that could later accommodate Jews fleeing out of Russia. This was really exciting! I had read Steve Lightle's book *Exodus II* in which he described his vision of Jews fleeing from Russia and being allowed to emigrate for the first time. These were prophetic events and their significance generated a lot of interest.

The Polish lady and I became friends. When she was in England again, she invited me to visit her in Cambridge, where she had been staying for two months looking after her daughter who was ill with cancer. She explained that she really needed to go back to Poland for a time, but needed someone to look after her daughter. When I heard this I felt an excitement within from the Holy Spirit, and although the reasons at the time were not clear, I felt that I should offer my services. My friend readily accepted and preparations were made.

On my first Sunday in Cambridge I went to the nearby Baptist church where I was struck by the subject of the sermon: "Go into the City and I Will Show You What to Do." It was as though God was speaking straight to me.

"What city is this?" I asked the Lord.

The answer impressed itself into my spirit: "Warsaw."

Warsaw was on the River Vistula. Now I had received, prior to this, a Scripture verse from a very reliable brother about the River Chebar (see Ezekiel 3:13–15). I had asked God which river represented the Chebar and He had said, "Vistula." *God must want me to go to Warsaw on the way through to Moscow*, I thought. Excitement flooded my heart! When I applied for my visa to visit Poland, it became clear why the Lord had wanted me to care for the Polish lady's daughter. My friendship with her was the key to getting my visa and entering the Eastern bloc.

Other Scriptures I had been given indicated I should take an overland journey rather than a flight, but I had no idea how I was going to complete the final stage and get into the USSR. I just felt from the Lord that I should set up the Russian part of the journey when I was in Poland. Everyone said this was impossible and I must organize it from England; but I knew that God was specifically telling me to wait and make arrangements from Poland. Obeying Him is always the key to success.

Remembering the line from Berlin to Moscow in my vision, I first went by train to Berlin. The capital city of Germany was of course at that time divided into east and west, with the infamous "wall" separating the two halves. When I arrived in West Berlin, a friend arranged for me to stay for two nights at the home of another lady, a doctor who spoke English. This gave me one full day to look around.

As I considered this, the Lord began to impress on me that I should cross over into the eastern section. My new friend explained what I needed to do. She showed me an underground station nearby where I could take a train, changing once before getting off at a station called Friedrichstrasse; from there I could get into East Berlin. She swapped my English money for German coins so that I could buy a ticket and then we parted.

Being English, I assumed that meant from a ticket kiosk, but in fact it proved to be a machine with instructions in German, which of course I didn't understand. A passer-by came to my aid and I went on my way, but soon found I was confronted by a choice of directions. Commuters jostled and made their way purposefully along the various passages and stairways. I asked the Lord which way I should take and felt impressed to go up the stairs to the left. At the top I approached two ladies for help, but they spoke no English. Trusting the Lord that I was doing the right thing, I walked confidently along the platform.

What happened next was amazing. As the train approached, a lady appeared – from where, I didn't know. She was dressed in a jade-coloured suit and was beautiful, with striking features, jet-black hair, and a lovely complexion.

She spoke to me in English: "Do you want to go to Friedrichstrasse? Come with me; I will help you."

We got on the train and sat together. After a few stops she led me off the train and took me to a branch line in the station. "This will take you to Friedrichstrasse," she said.

And then she was gone. I stood there for a few seconds, dumbfounded. *How did she know where I was going?* I thought. Much later I wondered if she had been an angelic messenger whom the Lord had sent to direct me. Such things do happen.

Crossing the border into East Berlin proved to be fraught with difficulty. Lengthy formalities and the stern expressions of the officials did nothing to make it either easy or pleasant. Eventually a pass was stamped and I was allowed to leave the station.

As if gaining access to another world, I left the station and entered the Eastern bloc for the first time in my life. What a contrast to the West! The drab architecture seemed not only to reflect the political system but also to complement the miserable faces of the people walking the streets. Everyone seemed to be plainly dressed. Everywhere there was a pervading sense of being watched. What a journey I was on!

I walked down the street, gazing at this strange part of the city. It was no doubt the Lord's way of introducing me to the communist way of life. Nothing seemed to have been repaired or painted for years. I discovered later on my journey that the further east one went, the worse the conditions got. There were no colours; nothing pretty at all. I was reminded of a garden shed that isn't painted regularly and eventually turns grey. This was East Berlin: grey, drab, nondescript.

I went into a museum. There was a sign explaining that in the period when people believed in myths and legends the building had been a church! I climbed up to the tower and when no one was around declared Jesus to be Lord over the city. I looked out at the scene before me which was intended to celebrate all that was humanistic and secular. I stayed for a little while to pray.

When I came back down I walked for some minutes, eventually coming to a park where I sat on a bench to rest. I had felt that eyes were watching me, but on this occasion I don't think I was actually followed.

Some people came and sat near me. Although one of them spoke English, he seemed very wary of talking to me. He didn't say much, but simply asked if I liked East Berlin. I truthfully told him it was my first visit so it was difficult to say. This was my first real understanding of how fearful people were in the East. They had been taught not to speak with foreign visitors because the authorities wanted to prevent their citizens from finding out what life was like on the other side of the Berlin Wall.

Feeling in need of coffee, I moved on from the park and found a café. Inside, everything was bare: no tiles on the floor; only wooden chairs to sit on. The coffee had an artificial flavour, but nevertheless was black, hot, and sweet.

A couple were sitting nearby and I smiled at them. When they smiled back I asked, "Do you speak English?" They didn't, so I drew the shape of a cross on the table with my finger. Suddenly their faces lit up and they beamed at me – I had found some believers! It is amazing how the connection between Christians transcends many barriers.

It was soon time for me to cross the border back to West Berlin. Somehow I got on the wrong train and found myself on the normal surface train but with an underground ticket. *What am I to do now?* I thought. But even here God sent me some help. A lady sitting nearby could speak English and when I explained the problem she said, "Come with me."

We got off at the main railway station in central Berlin and after she explained to the ticket inspector what had happened, he just smiled at me and let me through! The trouble was, I was now lost. I had my friend's home address of course but didn't know how to find it; Berlin is not a small city.

"No problem," my new helper said. "I have my car here." And bless her, she drove me back to my doctor friend's house. How I thanked the Lord for helping me! He never lets us down.

The next morning I took the train across the Polish border and on to Warsaw, where I was met by my friend, the mother of the sick lady I had looked after in Cambridge. She took me back to her home and after something to eat we talked about my onward journey.

To visit the Soviet Union in those days was a very formal affair. Tourists did not have the freedom of individual travel that they have now; it was necessary to be part of a tour group. Also I quickly found that people were again telling me that I should have made all the arrangements from England before setting out. At this point it would have been easy to become dismayed but it was a lesson in learning to trust the Lord, because I knew in my heart that, despite the usual protocol, God was directing me to make my travel plans from Warsaw. I believed the Lord had everything in hand, but apart from ending the journey in Moscow I did not know where else He wanted me to go.

My hostess took me to the travel agent. Thankfully, that morning in my prayer time, the Lord had given me further direction and I knew I was to visit the cities of Lvov and Kiev in Ukraine. (At that time, though, I didn't know they were in Ukraine; I thought the whole area was Russia.) The Lord also gave me two dates for each city, the purpose of which I just had to leave to Him to reveal in His time.

The travel agent confirmed everything others in Poland had told me. "You cannot join a tour into Russia from here," she said. We discussed the issue back and forth but she was adamant that it was not possible.

I silently threw a prayer skywards and pleaded, "Help me, Lord. You told me to do this!" Suddenly I found myself saying to the travel agent, "You mean I am *so* near and yet I cannot go and see Russia?"

She looked at me with pity, her eyes saying, *Why would anyone actually want to go there?* Then amazingly she blurted out, "Of course, I could arrange a *private* tour for you."

I was so relieved – God had had His way!

"Yes, please," I said and gave her the names of the cities the Lord had given me: Lvov, Kiev, and Moscow. These she accepted without question.

"Do you want to fly or go by train?"

"Umm, train please."

"Then you will have to go overnight."

"Oh no!" I protested. "I want to see the countryside."

She gave me more pitying looks. "Well, you can't. It's not allowed – you might see something you shouldn't."

Now I understood the significance of the two dates the Lord had given me. If I went by train I would leave in the evening (the first date) and arrive in the morning – the second date. God knew everything about this trip, of course. I had such a lot to learn!

It took a whole month to set up, going to the travel agent once a week; the "red tape" was unbelievable. The visa could not be obtained until hotels had been booked. The hotels wouldn't let you book until you'd got the visa. Each week we had to wait in queues and fill in lots of forms. There didn't seem to be any carbon paper, so each form had to be filled out four times separately and signed. Eventually everything was complete: the forms were given to the correct department and I was told to pay. This presented its own problem because I was told to queue up at yet another place. However, I couldn't pay here either, because I only had Polish money (not surprising as I was in Poland) and the clerk wanted to be paid in Russian money for a Russian tour. This entailed leaving the queue, going to a bank, and buying Soviet roubles. Then all the queuing started afresh.

Apparently this was the system: endless queuing up to tell people what you wanted, acquiring a chit for it, queuing up somewhere else to pay for it, and finally queuing up somewhere else again to collect your goods. The people stoically waited in queues day in, day out, the weariness of all this enforced patience etched on their faces. It was no good fretting about it; it was the way of their society, and it created jobs for people who had to service all the queues. It was the same in many shops. The communist states had no unemployment problem and it was easy to see why.

During the month I was in Poland I was taken to Auschwitz, which was a profoundly deep, emotional experience. I also went to the farm where the house to accommodate Jewish people was being built and where Bible camps were held in the summertime. Here I helped with the cooking and spent much time in prayer. Ten days had already passed and I prayed, "Lord, You said You would show me what to do . . ."

The very next day, a car arrived with two people from Jerusalem whom I knew. Jay and Meridel Rawlings, the authors of a book called *Fishers and Hunters*, who had travelled the world telling Jewish people that God was calling them home to Israel, were trying to get into the Soviet Union. They had been there the year before and had secretly made a film about the "refuseniks." These were Jews who had been "refused" permission to emigrate and were often beaten and imprisoned just for applying to leave. The film (and subsequent book) was called *Gates of Brass*. The Rawlings wanted to enter Russia again but had not been granted visas.

As we talked, it became clear to me why I'd had to wait for ten days to pass: it was to wait to speak to them. They had been shown by God that they would meet someone who would help them, someone He had put in their path – me! Jay and Meridel asked me if I would be brave and do something for them: they wanted me to take into the Soviet Union a suitcase full of clothes. It was destined for two Jewish families whose men folk had been imprisoned for applying to emigrate to Israel – or "make *aliyah*" as Jewish people call it. Apparently it was very difficult to get work on being released from prison, but these families could sell the Western clothes Jay and Meridel brought and generate some income to survive. I agreed wholeheartedly, wondering why they thought I was being brave. Little did I know!

Eventually everything was arranged and, in addition to the clothes, I agreed to take some Bibles, neatly wrapped and packed into my case. I was given contact details of the Jewish families I was to visit, as well as those of some Christian believers. The contact details had to be in code: only phone numbers with the message "I am visiting from England; do you have a church service?" In this way suspicion was reduced. I was also told never to take a taxi from outside my hotel, as this would guarantee my being followed and could endanger the people I was contacting. I must not loiter either, but just walk as if I knew my destination. Small denominations of money called *kopeks* would be needed for the public phones. I was told to be alert as the authorities would be constantly trying to watch my movements. It began to dawn on me why Jay and Meridel thought I was being brave. I felt like I was part of the "Secret Service" – and we all know what the Soviets did to spies. Ten years in Siberia did not appeal much!

I was driven to a town on the Polish/Ukrainian border called Przemysl (pronounced "Pshemish") where I was to catch the train into the USSR. I didn't get far, however, because I was forced to wait while officials examined dozens and dozens of photographs of women, comparing them with my passport photo and with me. An official then dismissed me and I had to go away and wait. Later another official summoned me and they went through the procedure all over again! Maybe they thought I was a spy. Eventually I was told I could enter the USSR and was taken to the train.

I didn't know I had been assigned a carriage and a seat (so the KGB could keep an eye on me) and not knowing what to do, I presented my ticket to a rather plump, angry-looking Russian lady on the platform. "Come!" she said bluntly. She took me to a carriage, showed me to a seat with a little table next to it, and again curtly said: "There!" So *there* I sat, and my cases were put in a little rack next to me.

When the train moved off, I got out a book to read and did some knitting for my grandchild to help me relax. After we had crossed the border a woman in a green uniform approached. She was accompanied by three or four soldiers with guns. She was very polite but firm and asked to search my cases. I had packed the extra case given by Jay and Meridel so I knew its contents – men's clothes, men's shoes, and a box of jewellery – but I wasn't aware that you were only allowed to take in clothes for yourself or that jewellery had to be declared.

The female officer, although happy that it was my first visit and that I didn't know anyone in the USSR, began to ask many questions. She continued her examination of my luggage and found the first Bible. At this, she seemed to freeze and her tone became icy too. "What language is this?" she asked, as if checking that I knew what I was carrying. The soldiers stood round me, aiming their guns at me as she began to pull out the rest of the Bibles. I began to shake a little and had to pray off the fear which gripped me so that I could appear relaxed.

At this point the Holy Spirit whispered, "Be truthful," so I replied, "Oh, it's Russian; they are Russian Bibles."

She seemed surprised at my honesty and then the questions continued: "Who do you know in the Soviet Union?" "Have you been before?" "Who are these Bibles for?" "Who are your contacts?" She appeared now to be convinced that I had contacts in Russia.

I said truthfully, "I don't have any contacts. I've never been to Russia before." Saying this once did not appear to satisfy her so I repeated it several times. Then a strange thing happened. I suddenly heard myself say, "I am going to learn Russian; my daughter is learning Russian and I have a Russian friend in England . . ."

I didn't finish the sentence but she seemed satisfied.

"Where did you get these Bibles?"

"Germany," I replied, before suddenly remembering that I'd got them in Poland. I felt uneasy at this because I knew the Lord had said to be truthful. But then the thought flashed through my mind: *Well, I believe the Lord is guiding me and He doesn't tell lies.* (All of this seemed to be in line with the Scripture in Matthew 10:19–20 which promises that the words you need to say will be given to you when you need them.) I later realized that the Bibles must have been printed in Germany and then brought into Poland because printing Bibles wasn't allowed behind the Iron Curtain.

Suddenly I heard myself say, "But I would have bought them in Moscow . . . but people told me that I would not be able to buy Bibles in Moscow. Can I buy Bibles in Moscow?"

She looked stunned. *What kind of idiot is this?* her expression said. She smirked, with a sarcastic laugh, and snapped, "Leave all those books on the table and sort out your cases." She and the soldiers then left the carriage.

While she had been going through one of the cases looking for Bibles and Christian literature, she had not, for some reason, noticed the forbidden items: the men's clothes in the second case. Tourists were only allowed to bring into the country personal items for themselves, but I didn't know that. Similarly there was the box of jewellery which I hadn't realized needed to be declared, and again the official hadn't noticed it. It was quite amazing. The Lord had it all in hand.

As I went to repack the cases, the other passengers smiled and gave me "thumbs up," but the Holy Spirit whispered to me, "Be careful . . . slowly." Keeping this in mind, I smiled and continued packing my case. I prayed that I would be allowed to keep the Bibles.

When the female officer returned she said, "You may keep them."

I was so relieved and began to pack the Bibles away again in their newspaper wrappings. I suddenly realized that it was Polish newspaper and that the official had failed to notice. It became apparent to me much later that the authorities had let me keep the Bibles in order to follow me and find out who received them, but thankfully this did not happen. God had it all worked out.

I soon learned how much I was being watched. My every move was under scrutiny. When my train arrived anywhere, I was met at my seat and accompanied to my hotel. Porters took my cases to my room. A "key lady" on the landing gave me my key and took it from me if I went out, noting down the time I left and the time I returned. When I checked out of a hotel, porters took my cases to the taxi, and I was escorted by someone to my seat on the next train. My ticket recorded the train, carriage, compartment, and seat number. The Soviets knew exactly where I was all the time. It was incredible.

Later that day we came to Lvov where I spent two nights. Walking around the city, I realized I was being followed. I kept seeing the same man everywhere I went; he was always leaning on a wall or reading a newspaper. He didn't know I'd seen him but it made me realize I would always have to be careful.

In Lvov I came across an old lady selling knitted babies' socks on the street. She looked very poor and the boots were made of such coarse wool that in the West we would never put them on a baby. Something in my heart stirred me to help her, so I approached her to buy some. Suddenly two soldiers with guns aimed at us came and stood between us, watching carefully what we did. I bought two pairs of these rough woollen baby socks, while the soldiers watched what money I gave her and the change that she returned. When the transaction was complete the soldiers lowered their guns, oblivious to the fear etched on the old lady's face. This was an even deeper introduction to the harshness of communism than I'd had in Berlin and Poland. Within me was a growing relief that I was soon to be moving on from Lvov.

We travelled overnight to Kiev. The compartments had four bunk beds, two each side; men and women mixed together. Under the lower bunks, which could be raised up, you put your luggage. A mattress, sheets, pillowcase, and towel (all thin and ragged but clean) were provided for a few kopeks, plus a grubby blanket to cover you. No one changed for the night, of course. A rather aggressive lady came to take the money and also brought round Russian-style tea in glasses. Sugar was available but no milk. As it was my first overnight journey in the Soviet Union it was all new to me and I had to guess what to do, watching and copying others around me.

When we arrived in Kiev I was once more met at my seat and escorted from the train to a hotel. At reception I managed to buy a tourist map which showed the centre of the city – the only part of Kiev that one was allowed to visit. I also bought a few postcards which I didn't need, but by doing this I acquired some kopeks for the public telephones – if I could get to a phone without being seen. The next thing I did was book a couple of tours so that I seemed like a legitimate tourist.

After the tour the next morning, I managed to leave the hotel in search of a public telephone. There were many, all fixed to walls out in the open. Feeling very scared in case I was being watched, I tried the first number I had been given. No one was in. I walked further on and tried again and again at other phones, with the same result. I made my way back to the hotel, my tummy churning, praying that the Lord would help me to be calm. I felt the Lord say, "After six o'clock." I could not eat anything and just lay on the floor praying.

After 6.00 p.m. I slipped out for a walk. When I was some distance from the hotel I looked for a phone – all the time being alert in case someone was shadowing me. When I made the call a young man answered. He spoke in Russian but I had to speak in English, asking if there was a church service.

Switching to English he replied, "Perhaps we should meet?" He was from the Underground Church! We arranged to meet by the nearby statue of Stalin; he would come out of the underground station carrying a newspaper so I could recognize him.

At the appointed time I made my way to the meeting place, wearing a red scarf as a sign (I hadn't realized this was something communists did!). The young man walked around the statue and then pretended to recognize me. Smiling, he greeted me in Russian and then very quietly in English said, "Come with me."

Down in the underground metro station, he whispered to me not to speak but just to follow him. We took two trains and a bus back to his home, which for him was very risky and strictly forbidden by the authorities, although I didn't know that at the time.

A group of six young people were there. They were so thirsty for spiritual things that they got me to sing many of our Christian songs so they could record them. They also wanted to know what life was really like in the West, having been told so many lies by their government. What was the Church like? Were we short of bread and potatoes? Was there really no sugar? Was rice rationed? They all spoke good English and had a gentle radiance about them as believers.

While I was there they phoned my Jewish contact for me and marked on my map where I needed to go, setting up what proved to be a real adventure. They then suggested I stay the night with them. This was forbidden and for them extremely dangerous, but as I was ignorant of the danger I did as they said.

In the morning they offered me breakfast but I had an urgent feeling that I needed to go straight back to my hotel. Georgi, the young man who had brought me, took me as far as he dared and I continued on alone. As I got near the hotel, the Holy Spirit warned me not to go straight in, so I hovered around outside pretending to check the numbers of the tour buses. After a short while I went inside; the two doormen stared at me as if wondering where I'd come from. I went straight in to breakfast and then up to my room, taking my key from the lady on the landing who amazingly didn't say a word. It seemed that no one had realized I had stayed out all night! God had covered the whole thing. As it says in Scripture:

> *He will cover you with His pinions,*
> *And under His wings you may seek refuge.*

(Psalm 91:4)

The next day I met a man called Ilya who had been at the meeting in Georgi's home. He gave me a bus ticket, took me to the bus stop, and said to count five stops and get off; from that point I was to follow the map. He would not come with me because they were having a party for a lady called Anna who had just been released from prison. She had received a five-year sentence just for typing a church notice. I wanted to meet her too, but the Lord spoke into my heart, "You are here on My business to help this Jewish family."

When the bus moved off I soon realized that I had a problem: I could not tell which the official bus stops were because the bus was constantly stopping and starting. I tried to follow the street names as best I could and suddenly realized we were going away from my route.

I got off and checked my map, recognizing a statue in the centre of the road. I started to walk but very soon realized I was lost. I could not match what I was seeing on the map with the streets! It seemed, from the broken state of the road and footpath, that I was out of the "tourist area." I had no bus ticket and could see no taxis. I stood still and asked the Lord for help. Nothing happened.

I said, "Lord, You sent me on this mission. I am not moving until You tell me what to do or send me help."

I waited expectantly, repeating my request to the Lord.

I felt impressed to cross the road, and as I did, I noticed tram lines just above the road surface. However, no tram had come by while I had been there. As I stood wondering what to do, some people began to emerge from a tall building. They were young girls, so I approached them asking, "Speak English?" I obviously scared them as they looked away and hurried on. I thought to myself, *What a terrible grip of fear the people of this country are in because of communism!*

More girls appeared and again hurried away, afraid to talk to a foreigner. Eventually a group stopped at my request and took the piece of paper I held out. As they were looking at the address, two older people appeared from behind a wall. They nodded to me, then nodded to the girls and took the paper from them, beckoning me to follow. Just then a tram came into view and it became obvious that this couple wanted me to get on it with them.

"Do you speak English?" I asked.

They just smiled. I had no ticket, but one of my "guides" seemed to know what I was thinking. He brought out a handful of tickets from his pocket and showed them to me, smiling. He spoke no words.

When we got on the tram the light was a little better and I clearly saw that these two "guides" were elderly, with shabby clothes and obviously very poor. The man had not shaved and was wearing a shirt with a frayed collar. I felt sympathy for these two whom I did not know. Why had they approached me in an area where I was lost? Why were they helping me? They didn't know who I was and why I was trying to find this address. A multitude of questions ran through my mind as the rhythm of the tram wheels rumbled in my ears. I offered them some English tea bags which I had been told Russians liked, but they declined with a smile. Still no words!

We got off when they indicated we should, and walked to another stop where we caught a bus. *I'd better give them some money*, I thought to myself, but just then the bus stopped and it was time to get off. We were at a main traffic intersection. There was another statue in the middle, similar to the one I had seen before – they were everywhere! I suddenly knew in my spirit that I was in the right place. I tried to tell my "guides" but they insisted on leading me further down the hill towards some buildings.

Then the strangest of things happened. It was as if some force was in charge of my legs. I inexplicably found myself walking boldly under an arch, through a door in a wall, and up a flight of stairs. The two people who had previously been my guides now followed *me*. This was totally bizarre as I had no idea where I was going! Though it seemed as if everything was OK, there was nothing tangible to indicate this.

We went up about three floors, each one with doors leading to apartments. Suddenly I saw on one of the door frames a *mezuzah*, the little wooden or metal compartment containing Holy Scriptures that

Jews put at the entrances to their homes. Excitedly I pointed to it, and my "guides" nodded and indicated that I should knock on the door. They stood one on each side of me while I knocked. The door opened abruptly – and a man grabbed me by the front of my jacket and pulled me inside, shutting the door.

I blurted out, "My friends – you've left them outside!"

To my amazement he spoke back in English: "Friends, what friends?"

"My friends – you left them outside," I repeated.

He just stared at me, puzzled. "You were alone," he said. "No one else was there!"

It was several days before it dawned on me that my "guides" must have been angelic messengers sent from God to rescue me and take me to this address. How else could they have known? I felt so bad that I had not been able to thank them and say "Goodbye," but the Lord knew.

The couple I was now visiting spoke very good English. They made me a cup of tea and we sat and talked. The main problem was that they wanted to learn Hebrew and go to Israel. The wife was a doctor and their son, Carmi, aged sixteen and a half, was due to go into the army at eighteen. Life for Jews in the Soviet Army could be very difficult and so this family were keen to go to Israel before their son was called up. If they waited until after his army service they'd have to stay for another five years, living in difficult circumstances. The husband had been learning Hebrew, and because of this and because he wanted to go to Israel the authorities had imprisoned him on a trumped-up charge. The KGB had arrived in the middle of the night, locked them all in the bathroom, and searched the apartment. They "found" drugs behind the clock and arrested the husband. His wife prayed and fasted for many weeks, and others around the world prayed. When the appeal was lodged, it was found that a mistake had been made and the husband was released. This was unheard of and had to have been the Hand of the Lord.

Because the husband had been in prison he couldn't get any work.

In addition, when their son Carmi was twelve years old a school teacher had called him a "dirty Yid" and incited the other boys to beat him up, leaving him unconscious in the street.

I explained that I had some clothes for them but didn't know how I was going to arrange the delivery. They suggested that I turn one or two shopping bags inside out, put as many clothes in them as I could, and put my coat over the top. I could then meet Carmi somewhere and he could bring them home.

We spent the afternoon talking about their lives and their hopes of going to Israel. Eventually Carmi took me to the main road and found a taxi to take me safely to the hotel. We arranged to meet the next afternoon.

The next morning I explored the city centre.

Coming out of the hotel, I walked down what appeared to be a main street: a dual carriageway with a central pedestrian area of trees and grass with occasional benches. It was not unpleasant, but whereas in the West the local authority would have planted flowers to brighten things up, here there were none. It was the same drab, colourless urban landscape that seemed to mirror physically what I could sense in the hearts of the populace, except in those of course who were believers. There were broad tree-lined boulevards with a fair amount of traffic, though not as much as in the West because most people could not afford cars and used buses.

I walked on, coming across huge tower-blocks of grey apartments that rose in clusters where communist architects with a mandate for function rather than form had provided accommodation for the workers. Looking at them, I imagined rows of cornflakes boxes painted grey.

The word "grey" seemed to be an apt description for both the colour of Soviet towns and the lives of the people existing under this satanically inspired regime. In addition, statues abounded of heroes of the communist system such as Lenin and Stalin. The purpose of this, presumably, was to emphasize to the workers how grateful they should be to the creators of this colourless society – a farce that could only be promoted by keeping people ignorant of the West!

This was particularly true in Revolution Square (every town had one of these) which celebrated the uprising that had brought in communism – the system which was supposed to solve all of man's problems.

I reflected on how successful it had been after I had looked at the shops. They had curtains or cardboard pictures in the windows so that you couldn't tell what they were selling, and once inside you realized why – they didn't have much to sell at all. What clothes they had were all quite similar, with colours and materials dependent on what was available that particular year. I learned therefore that you could tell by a person's clothes the likely year in which he or she had purchased them! You would see several people wearing the same type of shirt or jacket. The poorly made dresses came in only three styles, and the shoe racks had three types of shoe. If you didn't fancy any of them you were stuck. Needless to say, there was no choice of colour in the underwear section, and function was the ruling element of design! As one would expect, the lack of choice caused many to attempt to make their own clothes, though any attempt at entrepreneurship would of course have been quashed.

In order to blend in, I wore basic clothes and tied my hair in a way comparable to the local women. Westerners, however, did tend to stand out because their skin was in better condition due to a healthier diet, but there was nothing I could do about that.

Right through the heart of the city, bringing goods on large boats, the mighty River Dnieper wound its way south. It was like a wide aquatic motorway with long bridges linking the two banks, and was obviously an important means of transport. During the Second World War the Nazis killed many Jews on these bridges by tying three people together, shooting the middle one, and throwing them in so the other two drowned. The Jews had suffered so much anti-Semitism here.

I met Carmi that afternoon at 4.00 p.m. in the appointed place; he was dressed in his school uniform and smiling. We went back to his apartment with some of the clothes which I had smuggled out of the hotel in bags as suggested. No one had noticed me.

When we got to Carmi's flat his mother had cooked a lovely meal of chicken. It was delicious – one of the nicest I had in the USSR. Afterwards I mentioned that I'd like to visit Babi Yar, the place in Kiev where thousands of Jews were stripped naked and machine-gunned into deep pits over the course of a few days. Carmi agreed to take me, so we set off. The Soviets had put up a large memorial but there was no mention that it was Jewish people that had been killed; it was made to look as if they were just Soviet citizens of no particular ethnicity. When the Nazis started this killing they put notices up for three days that all Jews were to be in the square at 10.00 a.m. When they had assembled, the soldiers drove them with whips, guns, and dogs along the streets to Babi Yar just outside the city, where there were natural ravines. Here they were made to remove their clothes, and were shot and covered with lime. Old people and babies were thrown into the pits alive as it was considered a waste of bullets to shoot them.

As I walked through the trees at Babi Yar the strangest thing happened to me. The most awful arthritic-type pains went up my legs into my hips and I started to weep and weep. I said, "Lord, what is it?" and He said to me, "That is *My* suffering." The Lord was allowing me to sense some of the pain He experienced because of the suffering of His people.

Eventually I couldn't take any more and we had to come out and go back to Carmi's apartment. After a short while I said I needed to return to the hotel, so Carmi took me down to find a taxi. He had been such a well-mannered boy and such a good guide; I was very impressed with him.

When I got back to my room I lay on the floor and wept and wept and wept, praying that God would let this boy go home to Israel.

"Get him out, Lord, get him out!" I cried to the Lord.

Three days later the family got their visas! I didn't know this until I got back to England. I was only one of many, many people praying for them, and God had heard these prayers. What a heart God has for His people!

Before leaving Kiev I made contact with the "Underground Church" again. It was Sunday so they took me to one of their larger meetings. We met at the usual statue and I was led to a spacious church hall with many people already assembled. The old ladies were wearing headscarves and there were no children.

The meeting was of course in Russian, so a young man called Andrei who spoke English was assigned to help me. Part way through the service he said to me, "They want you to give them a message."

I was so surprised and didn't know what to say. I knew I had to be careful because the KGB possibly had spies in the church. So I stood up and said that I brought greetings from the West and that it was good to share the service and worship God with them. It was just a general kind of message, including greetings from my own church.

As I talked I got bolder and said, "The most important thing for all of us is to keep our eyes on Jesus because Jesus Christ is Lord. Jesus Christ is Lord."

There was a stunned silence because the believers didn't usually mention His Name, although I didn't know that. After the service ended they kept me at the back of the hall in a darker area. Then I was smuggled into a car and taken to somebody's house on the far outskirts of the city – I didn't know where it was – where they had arranged a meal.

This house, I learned, was the home of one of the pastors of a different church. He loved Israel and wanted me to tell him all about it. He also asked about the West and whether it was true that we had no potatoes – the same questions I had heard from others.

We had a long talk about Israel and then he said to me, "Do you have any Bibles?" I told him that I did. At this he got very excited. With Andrei translating for me, we arranged how I could deliver the Bibles. Andrei suggested I put them into a carrier bag (as I had done with the clothes), drape a jacket over it, and calmly walk out of the hotel. The meeting place was a nearby fountain. I should go there and sit on a bench; Andrei would come along with another plastic bag – full of rubbish – and sit next to me, putting his bag next to mine. We wouldn't speak but just appear to be resting. Then he would pick up my bag and walk away. A few minutes later I was to pick up his bag and leave, and so we would pass the Bibles undetected.

The plan went just as arranged without anyone suspecting anything. I was very relieved! Most people didn't own a Bible and the authorities had burned many copies. In fact it was illegal to have a Bible and so people kept them hidden, like secret treasure, which of course they were!

(Years later when the communist regime had ended, I found myself back at Andrei's church – and everyone had a Bible. It was wonderful! Praise the Lord!)

That night I was taken by an official to catch the overnight train to Moscow. As usual, when we arrived the following morning I was collected from the train compartment. My "escort" was a grumpy man, not at all pleasant. He took me to my hotel, which happened to be the International, facing Red Square. I was in a little room on my own at the back, which necessitated a circuitous route through many corridors to get to the entrance. I found my way out and looked at Red Square with the onion-shaped tops of St Basil's Cathedral and the austere walls of the Kremlin. I was astonished that my hotel was just next to this significant place. However, from the minute I arrived in Moscow I sensed a deep spiritual darkness. The atmosphere was horrible and the people unfriendly, and a dislike of the city settled in my heart.

I felt that, as in Kiev, it would be a good idea to arrange a city tour so I could get my bearings and be seen to be doing what was expected of tourists. The coaches took us all around the city past the various buildings and landmarks such as the university and the river. Then I decided I should go out on the street and look for the Jewish people. As before, I went some way from the hotel to find a phone.

When I dialled the number and spoke English I was answered in Russian and of course I didn't know what they were saying. This happened three times. On the third occasion I got a feeling of alarm. The person on the other end said, "Wait!" I had a horrible feeling they were going to get the line checked so I put the receiver down.

At the back of the International was another hotel with a tea shop where I could buy snacks (I was booked for only "bed and breakfast"). While there, I came across two ladies from England who were astonished to meet me. We got chatting and they asked if I was with a Christian ministry called Open Doors. I replied that I wasn't, all the while concerned that we would be overheard. They took my address and when they returned to England they contacted my family to let them know I was all right. This happened several times on trips and was a great help for my family as it seemed that periodically I disappeared into the "unknown." They were of course glad of any news of me.

The next day I decided I must try and visit the Baptist church so I got a map and took a taxi there. This was quite in order as this large Baptist church was a showplace to convince outsiders that the Soviet Union was a tolerant country. It was all a façade of course, which became clear when you looked a little deeper: all the churches in Moscow, apart from this Baptist church, one Catholic church, and one Orthodox church, had been shut! As only these three churches remained, everyone used to crowd into them. Unfortunately not a few Western visitors believed what the authorities were trying to portray through this façade.

I found the Baptist church and went in. There was a little kiosk just inside with some officials in it. I knew immediately in my spirit that they were not Christians. In fact they turned out to be KGB officials. One of them, a lady, told me this was where she got baptized, but I knew she wasn't telling the truth. It is a fact that the Holy Spirit in a believer recognizes Himself in other believers so it's not difficult to know when one is being lied to by unbelievers pretending to be Christians.

She proceeded to show me round the church and explained the services, commenting how full the church was. This of course was an attempt to convey how free religious practice was in Russia – all part of the deception. She neglected to mention the trumped-up charges that so often ensured long prison sentences for real believers. I asked her why all the other churches were closed and she didn't know what to say.

After she had shown me round, I explained I didn't know my way back to the hotel – was there anyone who could help me?

"Oh, yes," she said and signalled to a boy of about fifteen years old who could speak English, giving him instructions to take me back to the hotel. This boy obviously wasn't a KGB member and I felt safe with him. When we got outside I asked him if the synagogue was nearby.

"Do you want the synagogue?" he asked me.

"Yes."

"It's round the corner," he replied and took me straight there. As I hadn't been able to phone the Jewish family, I thought it might be a good idea to go there.

It was a huge building with tall pillars. I went up the steps. Inside there was a side room where some Jews were praying, and sitting at a desk was a man in a brown suit.

"Good morning," he greeted me.

I told him that I was looking for a family of refuseniks.

"Refuseniks?" he said. "There's no such thing."

The Jews who were praying were looking very nervous.

"Oh," I replied, "that's a shame; I've brought some clothes for them."

"What's their name?" the man in brown said.

I pretended that I couldn't remember but it was something beginning with "Rose . . ." I made up a surname of that sort.

"We haven't got anybody of that name."

All this conversation had taken place in Hebrew because the man didn't speak English; it prompted him to ask me where I had learned Hebrew.

"In Jerusalem," I replied.

At the word "Jerusalem" he became more interested, and the men who had been praying suddenly pricked up their ears and started to pay attention to us.

"Why don't you come back tomorrow?" he suggested. "I'll try to find out more about this and let you know."

I had just reached the bottom of the steps outside when a man appeared from behind a pillar. His head was shaved and he was incredibly thin. He looked very hungry and I realized that he had probably just been released from prison.

"Psst," he whispered to attract my attention. He then said in English, "I am a refusenik."

"Ah!" I responded.

"If you bring the things tomorrow, I will get them to the people," he said.

"That's wonderful," I replied. "Do you know how to get back to my hotel?"

"Which hotel is it?"

I told him and he led the way. He scurried along, using the narrow passages between buildings rather than the roads, and because he was so thin he reminded me of a rat. Every so often he looked back to make sure I was following. When we came to a road he would look right and left and then dart across in a nervous manner. Eventually we reached a tunnel leading into the Moscow underpass system as pedestrians do not cross the larger roads on the surface.

As we went along I remembered that I had with me a Hebrew Bible which included the New Testament, so I offered it to my unofficial guide. He started to jump with joy, kissing it, and holding it to his chest! He was so delighted.

Before very long we came to some steps.

"See you tomorrow," he said. I went up the steps and there was my hotel. I felt relieved and also joyful at meeting my new friend.

I had the afternoon free and decided that I would go inside the Kremlin where there were five old churches which had been turned into museums. Naturally, entry to the government buildings was restricted but one was allowed to walk around the outside of them which I did, praying everywhere. I also criss-crossed Red Square proclaiming the Lordship of Christ. It was so noisy in the square I didn't worry about being overheard. I shouted, "Let My people go!" and "At the Name of Jesus every knee shall bow!" No one took any notice of me.

Thinking about delivering the clothes, I went into St Basil's Cathedral (which I felt was a horrible place) and said to the Lord, "What am I going to do with these clothes? I don't have any more bags."

Into my head popped the words, "Go to the Bereoska shop."

The Bereoska shops were only for tourists. Russians were not allowed in, except of course for the higher-ranking members of the Communist Party. In these shops one could buy good-quality food and products from the West, but all very expensive and out of the reach of ordinary Russians. In addition, goods had to be paid for in Western currencies.

As I looked round I felt impressed to buy three attractive Russian dolls: one for my granddaughter and two for the girls on the farm in Poland. The sales assistant put them in two large "Bereoska Shop" bags. Back in my hotel room, I put the dolls in the suitcase and the clothes in the Bereoska bags, and hid the bags behind the door.

The next morning I had to check out and called for the porter to come and get my suitcases. When he arrived, he came right in and walked round the room for some reason; he noticed the bags but didn't say anything. I just knew that the hotel staff watched my every move and missed nothing. I went with him to the storage area and deposited my cases until it was time to leave.

After breakfast I fetched the Bereoska Shop bags. From the map,

I had found the street where the synagogue was, but had to ask the lady in reception to write it in English for me. She happily did so, but I noticed she put her other hand under the counter to press a switch, perhaps a bell. Everything was very amiable. I checked out and went to the door with my Bereoska bags. Near the entrance were two big men dressed in black, looking at me.

As I got outside and started walking, it felt as though a hand was placed on my back – but there was no one there.

"Lord, what's this?" I asked.

He said, "You are being followed – be careful!"

I prayed, "Lord, get rid of him. Tell me what to do. I don't want him following me."

The Lord impressed upon me to go down the underpass. Here the passage had two sides much like a dual carriageway. At first I went to the right but the Lord nudged my spirit to cross over and take the left side.

I still had the feeling of a hand upon my back, which I believed was the Holy Spirit showing me that I was still being followed.

"He's still there, Lord," I said.

I felt the Lord encourage me to keep going so I carried on. Eventually I noticed daylight illuminating some steps, and the Holy Spirit directed me to go up onto the street.

At the top I noticed a flight of steps going down again, and felt the Holy Spirit direct me to walk back down. There was quite a crowd of people going in all directions so I mingled with those heading into the underpass and suddenly noticed that the feeling of a hand on my back had gone. I took this to mean that I had lost the man following me. I was so delighted – praise the Lord! It was like an episode from a spy film, but I had the advantage of having God with me to direct my steps. How thrilling! God was in everything, watching over me and caring for me. I was filled with joy and asked the Lord, "What now?" When I got to the next set of steps I again felt the gentle nudge of the Spirit to go up.

On the street above were three taxis. It was a great mistake to take taxis from outside one's hotel because the drivers were always KGB agents, but elsewhere sometimes they weren't.

I asked the Lord, "Which taxi?"

Back came the reply: "The yellow one."

So I went to the driver, who appeared friendly, and asked him if he spoke English.

"Leetle, leetle," he said, indicating how little with his fingers. I showed him the paper with the street name.

"Oh," he said. "Big Jewish church there."

"Really?" I responded.

As we drove along I deliberately made conversation, asking about the weather and if he had been to England, but he didn't understand much. I then asked if he had any children. He nodded, so I offered him one of the children's jumpers from my bag. He was so pleased.

As I got out at the top of the street, I gave him quite a lot of roubles. I was leaving the country soon and wouldn't need them any more.

I headed towards the synagogue, looking all around for the thin little man who was to meet me and take the clothes. *Oh dear*, I thought. *Perhaps he hasn't got here yet.* I walked further up the street and back again several times, but he was nowhere to be seen.

"What am I going to do, Lord?" I prayed. I knew that if I carried on walking up and down with plastic bags I would be noticed and there would be trouble. By this time it was raining heavily. The thought came to me to go back inside the synagogue where the "man in brown" might help me. Little did I know!

Again I went boldly up the steps and into the synagogue. In the same side room there was another set of men praying and davening. Behind the desk sat a man in black who greeted me with, "Good morning."

The previous day the man at the desk had said he was the President of the synagogue so I asked this man in black if I could speak with the President.

"I am the President," he said.

"Oh," I replied, "I spoke with another man yesterday who said *he* was the President."

"No," came the firm response. "*I* am the President. What do you want?"

"Well, I was actually looking for a family of refuseniks."

"We don't have such people," he said.

"I've brought some clothes for them," I continued.

"We don't have refuseniks here. What's their name?"

I had another try at pronouncing the name of the family I was to get in touch with and noticed that the praying Jewish men were now frowning at me. The man at the desk started to ply me with questions: where was I from, who did I know, where was I going?

I replied, "Well, some friends asked me to deliver these clothes to friends of theirs, but if you don't know them I don't know what I'll do . . ."

Then into my head came the thought, "Ask to go into the synagogue." I'd seen it the day before so I knew that this time it was the Lord guiding me. So I continued, ". . . Oh well, perhaps I can just see the synagogue and I'll take the clothes back with me."

"Oh, you can see the synagogue," he replied and took me in. He started to point out the features and I admired it all, pretending I hadn't seen it the day before. Suddenly a phone rang and somebody called the man over to an office a little way off; he went inside and shut the door. This was all the work of God for as soon as he'd gone, another man appeared from behind a pillar and said, "Come, come!"

He led me round the side and through a series of rooms to a back office, where he took the bags off me. Then he moved some cupboards away from the wall, stashed the bags behind, and pushed the furniture back into place.

"Thank you, thank you," he said. "We'll deal with those; don't worry."

He took me to another door – and suddenly I was out on the street! It was still raining hard. However, as I'd come out of the synagogue on a different side, I didn't recognize my surroundings at all. "How will I get back to the hotel, Lord?" I prayed.

Once again, as had happened in Kiev, I had the sense that my legs were being driven by a force other than my own. It was peculiar. I felt myself walking to the left at quite a pace. I soon saw the Bolshoi Ballet which I'd noticed in the taxi on the way there, so felt reassured. I walked for quite a while, not knowing where I was going, but eventually headed down into the underpass system where I seemed to know whether to turn left, right, or keep straight on. Suddenly in front of me were some steps and I knew I had to go up them. There at the top was the side wall of my hotel! I had come back a different way. I was so relieved.

It wasn't quite time for me to collect my suitcases so I stood in the doorway wondering what to do. Opposite I noticed a long queue of people waiting in the rain to go into the mausoleum where the Soviets kept the embalmed body of Lenin. I had no desire to see it but I felt the Lord impress upon me to join the queue.

"No, Lord," I complained, "I don't want to go in there." But the feeling was so strong that I added myself to the slowly moving line of people.

Eventually we got to the security desk where we had to hand in our handbags, umbrellas, and overcoats. People were only allowed into the mausoleum one at a time, but as the lady in front of me walked with a stick and was unsteady on her legs, I went to help her and go in with her. A soldier with a gun stepped forward immediately and stopped me. The lady had to go alone.

As soon as I got inside I felt a great darkness enter my spirit, and a demonic buzzing noise filled my head. As I followed the circular steps downwards, it felt like descending into hell itself – it was awful. At each turn of the staircase there was a soldier with a gun. Everyone was expected to go down with great reverence, but I didn't: I prayed all the way, saying quietly, "Jesus Christ is Lord, Jesus Christ is Lord. At the Name of Jesus you shall bow the knee."

When I reached the bottom, people were gazing in awe at Lenin's body, which was in an armchair with his head and hands illuminated by lights. The buzzing in my head was louder than ever and I continued to repeat, "Jesus Christ is Lord, Jesus Christ is Lord."

The way out was up a different set of steps and we emerged right on the wall of the Kremlin. Now the Lord had shown me previously that I was to go from Berlin to Moscow but that I was to pray the other way: from the wall of the Kremlin to the wall in Berlin. I had wondered many times how I was going to get to actually touch the Kremlin wall, because I knew that the Lord wanted me to put my hand on it – and here I was, right beside it!

For about 20 metres I had to walk next to the wall, down some steps back into Red Square, so I was able to pretend that I was touching it to steady myself and pray while doing so. Down the steps I went, praying in "other tongues" (a phenomenon described in the book of Acts), commanding in prayer that the Jews be allowed to go free, and that the Soviet Union bow the knee to the Lordship of Christ.

Although to some people these actions may seem strange or even extreme, they were very specific prayers that I knew would have some effect in the spirit realm and would be significant in changing the decisions of those who were preventing Jews leaving for Israel.

When I got to Red Square a great peace descended on me – I knew I had done what God wanted me to do. I might have been dripping wet (it was still raining) but it was done!

Ladies with white overalls and hats were selling a kind of bun with hot mashed potato in it for about a rouble, so I bought one and ate it there in Red Square, glad to see that the rain was easing off. Then I found a hotel café nearby where I got myself a cup of tea and sat in the warmth to dry out.

By six o'clock I had collected my suitcases from my hotel and was at the station, only to find a problem waiting for me, or so it seemed. The carriage number stamped on my ticket was for a carriage that didn't exist! We consulted the man in charge who eventually found me an empty seat.

As the train left the station, an inspector arrived to check my cases. I thought, *I wonder what he's going to say when he sees only dolls in the suitcase, because he's bound to ask what was in the case when I entered the country.* I hadn't realized all the time that I'd been in the USSR that the reason I had been allowed to keep the Bibles was that they were going to watch what I did with them.

The man looked in the case and exclaimed in English, "Oh, you've bought some dolls!"

"Yes," I replied, "one for my granddaughter and two for my friend's children."

He thought that was lovely and began to tell me about his own grandchildren – in fact he was so friendly and chatty that he completely overlooked the obvious fact that the case must have had something else in it when I entered the country! He didn't ask at all. He didn't even ask about the other case that had contained the Bibles. Had I been put in the booked seat according to my carriage number, the officials might have asked what I had done with the Bibles. But the mix-up, which no doubt the Lord arranged, prevented this. God's protection was there whenever it was necessary.

Eventually the train arrived in Warsaw where my friends met me at the station, curious to know all that had happened. I stayed overnight with them, relating my adventures, and gave their girls the Russian dolls; they were thrilled with them as they had few toys.

The next day I got the train to Berlin, and as we were approaching the city, an interesting thing happened. I found that for some reason I got up and went into the corridor. A number of other passengers were there. Involuntarily, it seemed, I started to pray in "other tongues." No one took any notice of what I was doing so I prayed out loud, not really knowing why but just "moved" by the Holy Spirit to do so.

Suddenly I stopped praying and a great joy came upon me as if of freedom, like being let out of prison, and I realized that we had just come under the Berlin Wall. I knew then why the Lord had had me pray in "other tongues." The wall was an evil instrument of division that not only kept apart two very different ideologies and political systems but was also the means of dividing many families, so that some relatives in the east and some in the west were unable to visit each other.

I could only guess at what the prayers had been, but that they were warfare in the spirit realm I had no doubt. I had been praying against the symbol which epitomized so much evil.

For those who have never been led into spiritual warfare, let me assure you that prayer prompted specifically by the Holy Spirit is very powerful, and symbolism such as was represented by the Berlin Wall is very significant in the spiritual realm. (The Nazis used symbolism frequently in their own occult activities.) For this reason I knew that it was important to be totally obedient when the Lord impressed upon me to pray, and when He told me to go somewhere.

At Friedrichstrasse the train stopped. The Russian guards now had to leave and be replaced by German guards; no passengers were allowed to get off at that point. It seemed that every 2 metres along the platform there was a soldier with a gun. The train started again and before long arrived at the main station in West Berlin, where my friend met me and took me back to her apartment. I related to her how God had led me and indeed arranged for me to pray from the wall of the Kremlin to the wall in Berlin, with many adventures in between.

CHAPTER 3

ADVENTURES IN ODESSA

Some trust in chariots and some in horses,
but we trust in the name of the LORD our God.

(Psalm 20:7 NIV)

It was summer 1990. The communist world was in a state of collapse. The leadership of Russia was changing: the old guard had gone; a new era was around the corner. Satellite countries of the Soviet Union such as Poland, Hungary, and Czechoslovakia began to break away from their master.

Many people, Jews in particular, saw an opportunity so rare that it just had to be taken. Since the Bolshevik revolution of 1917 the people of the Soviet Union had been imprisoned behind what came to be called the "Iron Curtain." They were now free to leave if they wished and thousands seized their chance. Most first went to Berlin and from there to Vienna, which seemed to become a staging post for refugees. Their goal was various parts of the West but often America. For many Jews it was Israel. "*Hashana haba b'Yerushalayim!*" (Next year in Jerusalem!), the cry at the heart of every Passover meal, was now within reach.

The Lord was stirring my heart once more to return to the Soviet Union. "Go back there," the Lord was saying to me. "This time to Odessa."

What will I do in Odessa? I wondered. It was a new city to me and I didn't know anyone there. As I waited on God for further instructions, it became clear that it was to be part of a journey which included Leningrad, Moscow, and Kiev. I had visited these three places before, but Odessa was new ground.

"You'll have to help me," I said to the Lord – as if it could be any other way. I was completely dependent on His help all the time. "I have no contacts in Odessa," I told Him. "Besides, what am I to do there?"

Previously the Lord had directed me to take in Bibles and clothes. It had also helped that I'd been armed with phone numbers or addresses. This time I had nothing concrete, only a distinct impression that there was something special to be done there, involving a boat in the harbour, but at that stage I had no idea why. Going onto a boat in the harbour, I thought, would be off limits to foreigners and might even get me arrested! However, I knew the Lord was highlighting a harbour visit and I would have to wait to find out the details.

A few days later a friend called me from Berlin.

"Esther, we have lots of Jewish people camping near here," she said. "They've escaped from Russia and I've been talking to them. Two sets of people are from Odessa. Could you take messages to their relatives and tell them they're safe?"

So that is the Lord's plan, I thought.

"Yes, of course," I replied. "Give me the details and I'll do my best."

As a German she dictated the addresses as best she could, but she had the problem of conveying in English letters the sounds portrayed by Cyrillic script. The first attempt was unintelligible so we broke it down as a phonetic exercise, sound by sound. I still could not understand it all. However, I took what she gave me and said I would do my best to find these relatives and convey the message about their loved ones.

My younger daughter, Kay, agreed to come with me, and after visiting the other cities on the journey we finally arrived in the Black Sea port of Odessa. The weather was quite hot and the tree-lined boulevards offered shade as we walked along. Some of the old buildings in Odessa were quite attractive.

We found a beach where Kay "bumped into" some Jewish people who spoke English. She had a "knack" of making contact with Jewish people and this time found she had something in common as they, like her, were musicians. More importantly, she discovered that they wanted to go to Israel!

Very quickly we became friends and they showed us where there was a temporary visa office with long lines of people all anxious to leave the country while there was a chance. Many of these people were Jews, as our new-found friends pointed out.

They also showed us the wonderful Opera House and told us that there were many Jewish people there who were either singers or musicians.

It was an exciting time for us as we met so many Jewish people who were only too keen to go to Israel. They sensed a change in the political air – it was time to move while one could.

The second evening in Odessa, I knew we should try to find the relatives of the families in Berlin that we had messages for. We went into the street to find a taxi, but when I showed a driver the "addresses" that I had written down in English characters he didn't want to take us. This happened a number of times, which was odd. We obviously looked like foreigners, and for most taxi drivers foreigners meant money. However, all the men we asked just looked at the "address" and shrugged, before driving off.

It was commonplace for private car owners to stop and offer people a lift to make a bit of extra cash, but my daughter Kay was understandably very reticent about getting into a stranger's car. I had drummed into her from an early age that she should never do this, yet now she saw her mother suggesting it. But what could I do? It was now getting dark and we had no transport.

After we had prayed for several minutes, asking the Lord to send help, a white car stopped. The driver scanned the "address," indicated that we should get in, and then sped off confidently. As the minutes passed, it appeared we were leaving the city behind and heading out into the countryside. On and on we drove with darkness fast approaching.

Kay was getting quite nervous now and whispered to me, "Where is he taking us and how are we to get back?"

I didn't know the answer but tried to reassure her. I just had peace that all was well. I have to confess, though, that my peace became increasingly tested as time went on and we drove kilometre after kilometre into the dark, passing fields and forests, heading for an unknown destination.

After about forty minutes we came to an urban area where towering blocks of apartments stood in rows: the familiar Soviet-style monoliths, functional but not aesthetic. They were lit rather dimly and our driver, who spoke very little English, said merely, "Here, here," pointing at the buildings. He didn't know which one we needed but we thanked him profusely, giving him a large quantity of roubles for his time and trouble. He drove off, leaving us standing alone and not knowing how to find the address we needed. We didn't speak the language and were basically helpless.

However, as the Scripture says:

> The LORD your God . . . will never leave you nor forsake you.
>
> (Deuteronomy 31:6 NIV)

So, since we were there on His business, I simply asked, "Which block, Lord?"

I felt impressed to look at a huge, wide building opposite us. I knew that these blocks often held a thousand families; therefore the hope of finding the correct apartment was slim indeed. There were five entrances at the front, and from experience I knew that there would be another five at the back.

"Which entrance, Lord?" I asked.

My eye was drawn to the middle one, so we walked over to it and went inside. There were no names to guide us. We went over to the lift. There were twenty-four floors.

"Which floor, Lord?"

Into my mind came the thought "Fifth." I pressed the button and the old, creaking lift started.

When we reached that floor and stepped out of the lift we were faced with three doors side by side; no names and no bells.

Again I prayed. "Which door, Lord?"

Immediately I knew it was the middle one.

As I rapped on the door with my fist, my daughter asked, "How do you know this is the right one?"

I didn't answer her but started singing a Hebrew song: "*Heveinu Shalom Aleichem*" (We Bring You Peace).

We heard a rattling of keys, which was encouraging, and then the inner door being unlocked. The outer door opened, revealing a young man of about twenty-five, clad in a dressing gown and trainers. He didn't seem surprised to see us, greeted us in English (with an American accent), and simply invited us to come in as if we had been expected. He introduced himself as "Leonid."

I showed him the "addresses" we had and told him why we had come. At this, he became really excited and called an elderly lady into the room, telling her in Russian that the family were safe in Berlin. The *babushka* was his grandma, he told us. He then phoned someone else to give them the news and explained that the two addresses belonged to one family and that members from each address had gone to Berlin. He was so happy and pleased that we had come. He didn't realize what a miracle it was that we had found his apartment!

Typically, Grandma wanted to give us some food, which was the Ukrainian way of making guests welcome. The main item available at that time was fruit in the form of plums, which we had eaten frequently in Odessa. Sure enough, we were presented with a dish each of cooked plums while the young man, Leonid, plied us with questions about our visit to his country. He informed us that he was married with a new baby and was planning to leave for America as soon as possible. Unfortunately he didn't want to go to Israel.

Kay told him how beautiful it was there and I explained that God was calling the Jewish people back to their ancient homeland. However, he was convinced it was a dangerous place and said that his wife's parents would certainly not want him to take her there.

He asked where we were staying and said he was due to go into the city soon so would run us back in his car. It was so simple – we needn't have been concerned. I'm constantly amazed at how the Lord takes care of all the necessities when we are doing His will. He never lets us down.

As we travelled back to our hotel along the dark roads, I found myself asking Leonid if he knew of any way we could have a trip around the harbour. The question just came out of my mouth and took me a bit by surprise. He seemed to think it would be no problem and arranged to call us the next day.

True to his word, the next morning Leonid called and said he would pick us up at 12.00 noon. He arrived with his wife, whom he introduced as "Swety." We had of course to look as though we thought it a good name, which in fact it was – a shortened version of "Svetlana" and supposed to be pronounced "Svieta"!

Leonid told us that first we were going to lunch and then we would go to the harbour and get on a boat. He did not explain how.

We had lunch in the basement of a dimly lit restaurant and then drove to the gates of the harbour. Leonid stopped at the entrance to show his identity card to an official; we couldn't hear what he said. Kay and I were in the back of the car and had been told to keep quiet and not say anything. The official let us through without a problem and, after parking the car, Leonid went to buy some tickets. We joined a throng of overweight women laden with bags of food, pushing and shoving one another to gain a better seat on a boat which I later realized was a ferry.

It left its moorings, making its way between ships of all types. Emboldened, I went to the stern and took photographs. No one seemed to mind or even notice that I was praying throughout the trip. The crew members just smiled, as did the women with their shopping. It was quite incredible. Every type of vessel was there, including grey Soviet battleships, and not one person said I mustn't take pictures!

Eventually we left the other boats behind and came out into open water. In a short while we docked near to the beach and everyone disembarked. It was very hot and half of Odessa seemed to be there. The water was crowded with people paddling and splashing: the young children naked and the women clad in just about anything, mainly bloomers and odd bits of cloth. They took no notice of one another and just enjoyed the sun, sand, and water, which I noticed wasn't too clean.

There were a few rusty merry-go-rounds and swings which, despite their condition, were used enthusiastically by the children. Ice-cream vendors plied their wares, which we sampled, but it was more ice than cream; and the "cold" drinks seemed to be lukewarm coloured water. Eventually it was time to go. The return journey was just the same, everyone elbowing and roughly pushing one another, without a care but with no real malice intended.

I went astern again to take more pictures. Praying while I looked at the scene before me, I asked the Lord to make a way for ships to take the Jewish people back to Israel from Odessa. I had no way of knowing of course that in the future this would be God's plan for Gustav Scheller's organization, Ebenezer Operation Exodus – it just seemed the right thing to pray. Obviously, though, the Lord wanted this intercession to take place to prepare the way in the spiritual realm as it was an unheard-of thing for a Soviet ship to take Jews to Israel.

The first Operation Exodus ship, full of Jewish people, sailed from Odessa to Haifa two years later in December 1991. God knew why I had to pray in the harbour!

CHAPTER 4

CHANGES ON THE HORIZON

The mind of man plans his way,
But the LORD directs his steps.

(Proverbs 16:9)

It was January 1991. The annual Intercessors for Israel Prayer Conference in Jerusalem had just begun. There were 120 delegates from twenty-four nations. There would have been more but many had cancelled their bookings and some airlines had stopped flights to Israel because of the threat of war with Iraq. Saddam Hussein had invaded Kuwait and threatened war with Israel if the US-led coalition attacked. His Scud missiles could reach Israel without difficulty and there was a great fear that he would use chemical weapons or gas, as he had threatened.

In Jerusalem we had been equipped with gas masks and the hotel had provided rooms that were sealed against gas attack by covering the windows with plastic sheeting. Every private home was told to set up such a room.

During our second night at the hotel we were woken by sirens. It reminded me of my childhood during the Second World War. Grabbing our gas masks, we made our way to our appointed "sealed room." Once everyone was inside, the door frames were covered with brown sticky tape. We all followed instructions, putting on our gas masks and laughing at the way we looked. We couldn't speak but at least we could pray. It was hot and uncomfortable, and the masks smelled of rubber. Time seemed to pass very slowly . . . Two hours went by before we were told we could come out. This happened every night, but during the day the conference proceeded normally. There was complete unity among those who were present and a lot of intercessory prayer.

It was during this time that Gustav Scheller had the distinct impression that the Lord was telling him it was time to start bringing Jewish people back to the land that God had given them. He shared this with the other leaders and they felt it was from the Lord. Gustav then told the rest of us and explained that he would need a lot of help and finance for such a venture.

As Gustav shared with us, I sensed the Lord speaking softly to me: "This is what I want you to do: go and help him."

After the meeting I went to Gustav and told him, "The Lord is saying I am to help you."

He replied, "Oh no, I haven't got *you* to add to my troubles!"

I wasn't sure then whether he was serious or joking. Had I misheard? Had the Lord really said I was to help? In my heart I knew He had.

The Gulf War, as it came to be known, lasted for six weeks and ended at the start of the Jewish festival of Purim. We got used to the sirens and even the bother of carrying our gas masks everywhere. There was a great unity among the people in Israel, whether Jew or Arab, foreigner or local. Everyone had a common enemy and helped one another in a remarkable way. Israelis can be pushy and noisy, especially in queues, but suddenly a mutual caring blossomed overnight, which was wonderful.

Sometimes I would be seen carrying my Bible and a crowd would gather around me. "What is God saying?" people wanted to know. "Has He told you anything?"

It was strange to be surrounded by men and women I hadn't met before, asking me such things, and I read out comforting passages to try to encourage them. One amazing thing was that every day in Israel at that time the newspaper headlines featured verses of Scripture! To my knowledge this has never been seen in Britain or America.

It seemed to me to be very significant that the war ended at the start of Purim, a feast when Jews all over the world celebrate their deliverance from the evil schemes of Haman as told in the book of Esther.

Saddam Hussein had also wanted to destroy the Jews but it was clear that God was watching over His people. After the war, accounts emerged of amazing escapes which could not have been anything but miraculous. A baby was buried in the rubble of a building but the masonry had fallen in such a way that it had cocooned her; she was found asleep but unharmed in her little protective shelter called a *mamat* in Hebrew. Another family were unable to get into their air-raid shelter because they had lost the key. They stayed indoors and a Scud missile took the roof off the shelter where they would have been hiding! There were many such stories. In all, thirty-nine Scud missiles were fired at Israel and there was only one fatality. There was significant cause for an especially joyous Purim that year!

I returned to England, full of what the Lord had said at the prayer conference, particularly Gustav Scheller's message that now was the time to help Jewish people go home to Israel.

While the Gulf War was raging and the West was preoccupied, Russia took the opportunity to invade the three Baltic states in an effort to bring them back under her control. Tanks had been sent into the capital cities of Riga, Vilnius, and Tallin, but the people had bravely assembled around their parliament buildings to prevent the Russians getting access. Many were killed, and the violence stopped only when news reached the West; however, there was a still a lot of tension in the region.

A few months after I returned home, the Lord led me to go to these Baltic states and to Leningrad (now St Petersburg) to help beleaguered Jewish people. Because of the hostilities no one had been permitted to go there, but in April a tour group was allowed in, and I knew I should join it.

During free time on the tour, I intended to take aid to certain people for whom I had contact numbers and addresses. A Jewish group in London had given me medicines for needy children, and besides these I had clothing, shoes, and money to pass on.

In Vilnius, Lithuania, we visited the ghetto. A once-famous place, it was now haunted by its violent history. There was such an atmosphere I could almost hear the stamp of Nazi jackboots. During the German occupation, the Jews – men, women, and children – had been driven outside the city to a place called Ponary. They were terrified, made to run, whipped as they went, and chased by dogs. At Ponary a huge mass grave reveals the place where they were executed. A railway line was even diverted there to bring more Jews from other areas. It was such a painful place that I felt the ache in my legs return, as it often did when I was in places of mass murder. I found it hard to stand. Although Ponary was in the middle of a forest, there were no birds singing; everything was strangely silent.

In Riga, Latvia, I met the family of Mikhail, one of the first Russian immigrants to visit the distribution centre of Christian Friends of Israel in Jerusalem.[1] He spoke English and it was he who had taught me conversational Russian. Mikhail, with his wife and two-year-old son,

1. Christian Friends of Israel is an organization that blesses Israel with practical support and provides the Church with teaching resources about the Hebraic roots of the Christian faith.

were the first in their family to make aliyah. His father, mother, and brother also wanted to go to Israel but were forbidden by the Russian authorities because the brother was sixteen and about to do his army service. If they had to wait for him to complete it first, they would not be able to go for another five years.

Mikhail had told me, with tears in his eyes, how he longed for them to make aliyah as he did not want his young brother Piotr to suffer the same anti-Semitic abuse he himself had endured in the Soviet military. "It's terrible being a Jew in the Red Army," he said.

I determined to pray for a way to get them out.

(In fact, later on, the Lord put it into my mind to ask my Polish friends to help achieve this by inviting Piotr for a holiday. Once in Poland he could head straight for the Israeli Embassy in Warsaw and ask for help to go immediately to Israel. It was a risk but I believed it was God's plan.

Mikhail's mother accompanied Piotr using the same invitation. Their main fear was being searched at the border. They could take only a few belongings or they would arouse suspicion. In addition they had to carry documents for the Israeli Embassy to prove that they were Jewish. If these were discovered, Piotr and his mother would no doubt be stopped. Mikhail kept me informed, and on the date they were to make the border crossing I asked the leaders of Prayer for Israel, plus some others, to cover that time with prayer.

On the day of the crossing, it appeared that everyone else had been searched but Piotr and his mother had walked through unseen. It was miraculous! Within a fortnight they were in Jerusalem, and since then the rest of the family have made aliyah too – father, grandparents, cousins, everyone. Hallelujah!)

I managed to deliver all the items I had to the correct addresses, encouraging the Jewish people I met to go to Israel as soon as possible. Some were enthusiastic, others less so, saying things like, "Oh, things will get better here, you'll see. We'll be all right." Their remarks reminded me of the time between the two world wars when Jews saw the political situation deteriorating in Germany and had time to get out of Europe but dismissed the signs, telling themselves, "Things will get better." It was a chilling reminder of what can happen when one ignores warnings.

The medicines I had were for a Jewish school in Tallinn, Estonia. I had a phone number, and the man I spoke to said he would meet me outside my hotel. We agreed on a code sign in case we needed further contact: the question "Will you come and have tea with me?" He gave me the registration number of his car, which was yellow, and told me his name was Sasha.

I was sharing a room with a lady called Barbara, who was not a believer but just a member of the tour group. It had been quite difficult to carry out my assignments without arousing her suspicion, and this time was no different. I left our room saying that I was going for a walk.

At the appointed time, I went outside and to my horror saw that all the cars in sight were yellow! I walked up and down the pavement looking at the registration numbers, trying to pick out Sasha's. Back and forth I went, asking every man who happened along if he was Sasha. "No," each one replied, which was quite remarkable as it had always seemed to me that "Sasha" was one of the commonest names in Russia.

I prayed for help as usual, and another yellow car appeared with the driver sporting a cheery smile. This was the right car. Sasha told me he had called the hotel to say he would be late but had not been able to get an answer. I fetched the medicines and other gifts and he was delighted with them, as the children, although cared for, lacked certain vital supplies.

I wished that I could have gone to see the children but this was not possible. Although the communist regime had come to an end, personal freedom had not yet worked its way through to every part of the former Soviet Union (fSU) so people had to remain careful.

Back in the hotel I found Barbara quite indignant.

"Do you know what happened?" she asked. Without waiting for an answer she went on, "A man had the cheek to call here and ask if I would go and have tea with him! To think that anyone would try that on with me!"

I remembered the coded message I had agreed with Sasha and fought back a grin.

When going into the fSU in those days, one had to declare how much currency one was bringing into the country and also on departure declare how much one was taking out, giving account of how the money had been spent. I had quite a lot of US dollars with me, destined for different people and concealed in my shoulder bag underneath a specially fitted piece of cardboard which served as a false bottom. It was dangerous to carry large amounts of cash, but this was what the Lord had provided to help anyone who might want to go to Israel. I only used the money as the Lord directed, and thankfully there was still plenty left as I found I needed it in the next and last place I was to visit on the trip.

Leningrad was a much polluted city. The tourist area was kept in better condition than the back streets which were another story: dirty, full of potholes, muddy water, litter, shabby buildings, and drunkards. My tour group had tickets for the Ballet Rombert but to everyone's amazement I declined. I had a job to do – find Jews. With only two days to go, I could not waste time.

After Barbara and the rest of the group had left I lay down on my bed. I had no contacts in Leningrad and so said to the Lord, "I don't know where to find the Jews."

His reply was, "Well, you won't find them lying on the bed. Go out and find the synagogue."

Downstairs I obtained a map and after a few minutes found a

symbol that looked like a mosque. I asked at reception and was told it was the "Jews' church."

I set off. Having travelled quite a lot in the fSU, I knew how the underground system worked. With the map to guide me, I made my way to the synagogue by metro and on foot. The "on foot" part became problematic at times as I had to negotiate my way past large groups of drunken men, while dodging puddles of dirty water with my head down so as not to attract attention. What's more, it was raining and I had no umbrella.

I found the synagogue – a large, fairly new-looking building – but unfortunately it was closed.

"Oh, Lord," I complained, "it's shut. I've come all this way and it's shut." At this point I was quite miserable, wet, and cold.

Quietly, the Lord spoke into my heart, "Go round the back."

I did so and noticed a rough driveway leading to another building where a man was loading up a van. I approached and asked in my newly learned Russian if there were any Jews there. (This building, I later learned, was the original synagogue.) The man nodded and indicated that I should follow him.

We went inside and up some stairs, and suddenly it was like stepping into a picture from an old Jewish storybook. There were several orthodox men gathered there wearing *talleisim* (prayer shawls), but my eyes were drawn especially to an old man sitting at a table, eyeglasses perched on his nose. Using a pointer, he was rigorously studying the pages of a book, maybe a Talmud, by the dingy light of a table lamp. He had thin white hair and a long beard. As I directed my attention to him, I became aware that the other men were gazing at me.

Emboldened, I said that I was looking for anyone who wanted to go to Israel. They all answered together, "Moishe" (Moses). Very helpfully, one of the men went to a phone and called this Moishe who, happily, spoke English. The line was bad and kept breaking up so there was a lot of repetition in the conversation. The men seemed unperturbed so this was probably nothing unusual.

Moishe said that he did indeed want to go to Israel but could not talk on the phone, so we should meet the next morning at my hotel. I left the synagogue and made my way back, feeling more cheerful in spite of the rain and the dirt.

At the appointed time I went down to the hotel lobby only to find it packed with tourists waiting to join various bus tours.

Where is Moishe? I wondered.

I looked carefully at all the people. They were Westerners, clearly: dressed in fine clothes and obviously wealthy. Then I spotted him behind a pillar – a small man with a large, dark beret pulled well down over his face. He had his head lowered as if he was trying not to be noticed, which in effect made him more noticeable.

"Moishe," I said, "I'm Esther," and held out my hand.

He was surprised and asked how I had recognized him – as if it wasn't obvious. He said that we ought to go outside to a park where it would be quiet and safer. We were soon settled on an old bench.

"Now, Esther," he said. "What is this all about? Why did you want to see me?"

I proceeded to tell him that I represented many people who loved the Jews.

He stopped me for a second. "Love the Jews?" he queried. "Love the Jews? No one loves us. People hate us. I don't know why." He hid his face behind his beret and then peeped shyly out from one side. "Maybe it's just you?"

I assured him that there were thousands of people worldwide who loved the Jews, and mentioned all the organizations I could think of that help Jewish people. He was silent as he thought about all this. I asked him if he wanted to go to Israel.

He said to me, "My grandfather wanted to go to Israel all his life. My father wanted to go to Israel all his life. And all my life I have wanted to go, but I cannot."

"Why not?" I asked. "It's possible now."

"You don't understand," he replied. "I used to work on scientific projects – secret things – and the authorities are worried that I might pass on information. They will not let me leave. My wife can go, my children can go, my brothers and the rest of my family can go, but I cannot." He stared at me as if looking for an answer to this problem.

"What was secret about your work?" I asked.

"That's the secret; no one knows! I retired fourteen years ago and we knew we were three years behind the West then, so what is so secret?" He shrugged and added, "I cannot wait alone here while my family makes aliyah." Sadness was written on his face.

"Moishe," I said, "I have news for you. If you go as a tourist you can stay there and get your papers done in Israel."

He wasn't convinced, however, and said that in any case he had no money for airfares.

"Moishe, I have money. The Lord has provided money for people like you."

He was speechless. He simply couldn't believe that Christians would want to help him, a Jew. He had never heard of such a thing and asked me why we helped Jews. I briefly explained that Christians owe a great debt to the Jewish people because from them came the Bible – and more importantly our Saviour, who was born a Jew. He wanted to know more, saying that he knew nothing about Christianity, and suggested that perhaps if he got to Israel I could teach him.

"Are there religious Jews like me in Israel?" he asked.

I assured him that there were.

We arranged to meet again the next day at his home so that I could give him the money discreetly. It was a long journey by metro and by bus. As soon as I entered his home I realized just how religious he was. He was very orthodox. I wondered what his friends would say if they knew he wanted to learn about Christianity!

I cannot remember exactly how much I gave him but it was enough to share with another man who was in the same circumstances. Moishe held the dollar notes as if they were holy, and assured me he would use them wisely. I knew he would.

When I returned to Israel later in the year, I called at the offices of Christian Friends of Israel, where I was a volunteer. There was a note for me. It said: "Esther, we are here. I will contact you when we have found somewhere to live." It was from Moishe.

Joy flowed through my heart to know that the Lord had done it despite all the difficulties! He had sent me all the way to Leningrad and used me to find this man and be instrumental in getting him and all his family to the Promised Land. How much God loves each one of us! (In fact I didn't hear from Moishe again but rejoiced in the knowledge that he was home in Israel.)

Later that year the Lord began to show me that I should leave Israel and that He had new plans for me. I wondered if they would be connected with Gustav Scheller.

CHAPTER 5

THE SAILINGS BEGIN

My purpose will be established,
And I will accomplish all My good pleasure.

(Isaiah 46:10b)

In the end it took about eighteen months to establish a shipping line from Odessa in Ukraine to the port of Haifa in Israel. Gustav Scheller, head of Ebenezer Operation Exodus, had chartered three sailings already but it was a momentous occasion when a regular route was set up. Never before had there been a direct route from what used to be a Soviet port to Israel, and this was made more amazing by using what had once been a Soviet ship. It was historic!

The ship was named after the Russian composer Dmitry Shostakovich, which was perhaps apt as there surely must have been music in heaven as the first *olim* (new immigrants) set sail to the Promised Land!

It had been a great struggle to get this route open and much prayer had gone into the battle, but it also took very determined servants of God – Gustav and his wife, Elsa – to bring it about. Gustav was tenacious and when he knew what the Lord wanted he displayed the British bulldog spirit, even though he was Swiss! He didn't give up until the goal was accomplished. God knew it would take such a man, and people knew that God's mark was upon him and that he had been raised up especially for this work. A lesser person would have given up.

Back in Britain the Lord had spoken to me about going back to Ukraine. I was to tell the Jewish people about the possibility of a ship running from Odessa to Haifa and that they should prepare to leave. I felt a little like Moses when God told him to gather the children of Israel and tell them He was going to deliver them from Egypt!

> Then Moses and Aaron went and assembled all the elders of the sons of Israel; and Aaron spoke all the words which the LORD had spoken to Moses. He then performed the signs in the sight of the people. So the people believed; and when they heard that the LORD was concerned about the sons of Israel and that He had seen their affliction, then they bowed low and worshiped.
>
> (Exodus 4:29–31)

About the same time, I met a lady called Shirley from the UK whom God had also spoken to, and it became clear that we had been given the same task and should go to Ukraine together. Travel arrangements were made: Shirley went ahead of me to find an apartment for us to stay in and I followed a little later.

Our first days were spent visiting Jewish people in their homes. It seemed, however, that some were doubtful that what we were saying about ships taking them to Israel was true. Others were more interested in going to America!

Sometimes we were invited for a meal, and in such situations we always took along a *menorah* and some candles. Often the family wouldn't quite know what to do with these items so we had to show them. Imagine that – two Gentile women explaining to a Jewish family how to use a menorah and candles! God hadn't wasted the years I'd spent in Israel.

Among the places Shirley and I visited were an orphanage and the children's prison. It is hard for Western minds to contemplate the existence of a children's prison but there it was – for children involved in petty street crime. The youngest child was only eighteen months old and had been found wandering around homeless. The authorities had had nowhere else to send him while they traced his parents.

The boys' heads were shaved and the girls' hair cut short because of lice. The poor things had nothing, so whenever we went we took them sweets but had to watch how they were distributed so that every child got the same amount!

Gustav and Elsa also visited them and at Christmas sent a box of bananas and oranges – foods which they had never eaten. The orphanage was a little more homely but only a little, as the ten boys and six girls aged twelve to fourteen slept in narrow bunks stacked three high in tiny dormitories. All the laundry had to be done by hand so we gave the staff money to buy a washing machine.

We did not know enough Russian to teach the children much about the Lord. Neither did we have an interpreter, but in simple terms we conveyed the fact that they had a Heavenly Father who loved them. We also taught them several songs with actions they could perform along with the words. I shall never forget the large eyes and pale faces of the children as they closely paid attention. It was such a moving experience.

Apart from making these visits, Shirley and I were engaged in a lot of spiritual warfare, especially in the dock area as this was where the ship would start from. The infamous Potemkin Steps were here, where Jews had been machine-gunned during the Second World War. Places where such atrocities had been committed were important places for us to pray. We were shown one area just on the edge of the city where during the war 24,000 Jews were rounded up, sprayed with petrol, and burned to death, children included. Our minds found it difficult to take in the horror of such events.

In February Gustav came out to Odessa and contacted us to say that the sailings were definitely starting before Passover in April. This is

recorded in his book *Operation Exodus: Prophecy Being Fulfilled*. This
was wonderful news and we could forge ahead with certainty.

I returned to England for a short time to reconnect with my family and
supporters. Waiting for me at home was a letter from the Ebenezer office
to formally invite me to join other volunteers for the sailings. Hallelujah!

> *Surely the coastlands will wait for Me;*
> *And the ships of Tarshish will come first,*
> *To bring your sons from afar . . .*

(Isaiah 60:9a)

In March a large group of volunteers, including myself, flew to Kiev
and then travelled to the Ebenezer base in Odessa by bus. For most of
these people it was their first time in the fSU and therefore somewhat
of a culture shock!

The Ebenezer base was a former communist youth camp for
youngsters aged about twelve to fourteen years, and an initial problem
was that the beds were an inappropriate size for adults – and likewise
the food portions! The beds caused a laugh or two for the taller ones
among us, but the food portions were more of a problem. Thankfully
they were eventually made a little more generous.

It was important to bring the olim to the base a few days before the
day of sailing to allow time to explain the immigration and customs
processes and tell them exactly what was going to happen to them.
The older ones among them would no doubt have memories of being
rounded up during World War Two and we didn't want to cause them
any anxiety.

The olim had a large luggage allowance of 250 kilograms each – far
more than if they were leaving by plane – and it had to be packed into
large wooden crates called *yarshiki* before being loaded on the ship.

Our first problem was that there were no yarshiki available! We prayed and prayed, and a supply of wood, nails, and tools was found. The men got together and began building the crates, but the uppermost question in our minds was whether they would be ready in time. And would there be enough? We had only forty-six olim for this first sailing so we were hopeful. The ship was due to arrive in Israel before the Passover holiday when Haifa port would shut down, so any holdups leaving Odessa would cause problems at the other end. Sure enough, the DIY crate-builders pulled all the stops out and managed to build everyone a crate in time.

However, the luggage problem was not the only one we had to cope with as we discovered there was insufficient fuel on board for the journey. Again we prayed and again the Lord sent the answer – more fuel arrived.

For just about every sailing there were problems, some of which seemed insurmountable. It seemed, as with the Israelites in Egypt, that the Enemy was doing his best to prevent the Jewish people leaving Ukraine. However, as the Scripture says, "At the name of Jesus EVERY KNEE WILL BOW" (Philippians 2:10), and with prayer the answers did come and problems were solved, sometimes at the last minute! It was wonderful for the olim to witness this. They knew we were Christians and were praying about these difficulties and so it was a great witness to them when the answers came. It also encouraged them to know that God was with them and was helping them. They would often comment to one another about how we had been praying over a particular problem and God had answered our prayers. The volunteers were not allowed to talk directly to the olim about the Lord Jesus as Gustav had had to give assurances to the Israeli government that we would not use the ship as a cover for Christian missionary work – something the Israelis were very concerned about.

Among the olim were several children and we had to cater for their needs in a special way. Obviously they couldn't be expected to spend three days on board ship with nothing to do – or further problems might have ensued. So we put on some activities for them and provided drawing and colouring equipment, as well as play dough and jigsaw puzzles. It wasn't long before the parents and grandparents were absorbed making models and doing jigsaws while the children played with balloons!

I was privileged to be involved on several sailings but also had times on the base when the teams changed over. These duties involved collecting olim from their homes or from the bus and railway station. Some of these people lived in appalling conditions up rickety staircases where there was little light. We carefully carried their belongings down and loaded them into the van to be taken to the dock.

At the railway station the trains were often unbelievably long and we'd have to wait until the whole train drew in so we could find the carriage we wanted. In the early days we had no trolleys either and had to carry the luggage by hand; it was hard work going backwards and forwards many times. The porters would try to extort money from us but because of the amount of luggage we sometimes had to use them. The weather too could be difficult: there would be thunderstorms which would soak us through, followed by strong sunshine which would dry us out! It was all quite a challenge.

The port terminal building was being revamped, and the process of checking the luggage was being done amid the dirt and dust of the building work. Everyone got filthy and often we would get back to the base to find that the water had been switched off until midnight. But the poor olim! Some of them had been on the train for two or three days and, being desperate for a wash, would go down to the beach for a swim!

At first the volunteers had no food provided at the docks and would have to remain hungry until they returned to the base. One day, as we weren't allowed into the hall where the olim were having their goods checked, two of us decided to have a walk, and found a restaurant. It was wonderful and we had some delicious *borscht*, the famous Ukrainian soup made from beetroot. Thinking of the men in our group whom we had left to guard the bus, we bought what looked like tasty pasties and took them back with us. There were no paper bags so we had to carry them in our hands. The men looked at them delightedly but when they took a bite their faces suddenly changed – the filling was cold fried cabbage and the pastry was like cardboard! We did laugh!

The evening before each sailing we held a social gathering: a chance to sing a few songs and give final instructions to reassure everyone. The olim called it a "spectacle"! We taught the children some Hebrew songs and a dance or two, and invited anyone else to contribute if they wished. Sometimes a person would come forward with a poem or a song or a reading. We always had a Bible ready with some appropriate verses. Most of the olim had never seen a Bible before and were in awe of it. A silence would fall while it was being read, and one or two shed tears as they realized what God was saying to them.

A touching moment came when the volunteers gave testimony as to why they were giving their time to help the Jewish people. Very often the olim would respond with comments like, "No one has ever loved us as you do," or, "We've known Christians all our lives but they weren't like you." More than once an elderly man or woman with a stick came limping out to the front and, barely able to stand, would say, "Maybe your Jesus is our Messiah after all." They would all applaud in agreement, yet we hadn't mentioned His Name.

On the morning of sailing we would accompany the olim to the port with their hand luggage. Their crates were loaded into the hold separately, direct from the customs shed.

Then there would be a customs inspection just before boarding. This could be a difficult time for the olim as the inspectors would take most of the jewellery that they found, allowing each person to keep the equivalent of about 7 grams of gold. The volunteers weren't allowed to take it on board for them either. Most of the olim knew about this and hid their valuables, but it was a heartbreaking process for one old couple who had been married for fifty years and had everything confiscated apart from one ring. The wife lost her earrings and Star of David necklace, and the husband lost his ring and watch. They wept, and we wept with them.

After three months the work period for most of the volunteers had elapsed and a German group arrived to take over. Building on the foundation we had laid, they improved many things. They repaired the wiring in the base so that appliances were less dangerous and more reliable. They also acquired some trolleys for moving luggage, and the meals were improved so that people had an adequate supply of food for the work they were doing.

Gradually the number of olim increased each month. We realized that it had been a blessing having a small number on the first few sailings as it had eased us into the program. If we'd had hundreds of olim, as we did later on, we would have been swamped and would have struggled. The Lord knew – hallelujah!

Word spread among the Jewish community that going to Israel on the Ebenezer ship was a good idea. By the twenty-fifth sailing, which Gustav and Elsa joined, we had so many olim that there was no room at the base and extra accommodation had to be found. Some of the volunteers crowded twelve to a room, which caused much laughter.

It had not been an easy start, but with perseverance, under God's guidance, an historic shipping line had been opened to take God's chosen people to their Promised Land. It had been my privilege to be part of it.

It was time for me to return to the UK. As I reflected on all that I had done and learned, I realized that everything we do in God's plan is not wasted but used as a preparation for the next step. If you are available to be used by God, don't be surprised at what you find yourself doing. We serve an amazing Almighty God. Nothing with Him is impossible, as I found out!

CHAPTER 6

AID TO ARMENIA

If a brother or sister is without clothing and in need of daily food, and one of you says to them, "Go in peace, be warmed and be filled," and yet you do not give them what is necessary for their body, what use is that?

(James 2:15–16)

"Esther, there are Jews there!"

It was February 1994 and my friend Hannah had just returned from one of several trips she had made to Armenia, taking Bibles, Christian teaching materials, food, and other aid.

"The situation is extremely bad," she continued. "There's electricity for only one hour a day, and food and fuel are in very short supply. The people are suffering, including the Jewish community. They need our help."

This kind of scenario was not new to me. I had been working for some years, as the Lord directed, taking aid to Jewish people in communist lands. I had also had recent experience working for Ebenezer Operation Exodus. I felt a stirring in my spirit and knew that I should give this consideration.

As a country, Armenia has an interesting but volatile history. It was the first entirely Christian nation, having adopted the faith in AD 301. However, during the period of the Ottoman Empire, it had come under attack by the surrounding Muslim states in an effort to create an Islamic region stretching all the way to China. The Turks, along with the Azeris from Azerbaijan, adopted a policy of ethnic cleansing and murdered up to one and a half million Armenians during and just after World War One.

Stalin's Red Army put a stop to this but implemented a policy of "divide and rule." This meant that some Armenians were moved to Azerbaijan, while some Azeris were moved to Armenia and Nagorno Karabakh.

In 1988, as the prospect of freedom loomed during the Gorbachev era, the people of Nagorno Karabakh called for a decision to transfer the area back to Armenia. The Azeris were furious and ethnic cleansing began once again. Murders and atrocities of the most appalling kind took place, including gouging people's eyes out and killing children by burning them alive or throwing them under moving tanks.

Pipelines carrying vital oil and gas supplies were destroyed, leaving Armenia with almost no fuel to face the severe winters. Daily life was extremely difficult for the population. There was almost no public transport and very little traffic on the roads. When they had to go somewhere, almost everyone walked.

In addition, electricity was supplied for only one hour a day and water was rationed because electricity was needed to pump it into the "high rise" Russian-built apartments. Food was scarce since there was only one international flight each week from Paris, plus one or two others from Moscow. Armenian winters could be severe and the apartment blocks were exceedingly cold.

An Armenian pastor named Ashot had explained all this to my friend Hannah. He complained that Christians from the West took Bibles into Russia but no one ever came to help the Armenians. He was studying in a Bible school in England and was very worried about his wife and two children back home. They were facing a winter where the temperatures could go down to -20° Celsius! Believing the Lord had called her to get involved, Hannah had taken aid to Armenia already by using the weekly international flight from Paris. Now she was organizing a ton of humanitarian aid and Christian materials to go by cargo plane.

All this exerted a pull on my heart but when she said, "Esther, there are Jews there!" and showed me photos to prove it, I felt an inner prompting from the Holy Spirit – I should go with her to manage the aid and see if we could help the Jewish population.

As it was winter, deep snow delayed our flight and also the planes loaded with aid. We took as much food with us as we could, including chocolate and fresh bread – and a bag filled with boxes of eggs which I carefully guarded all the way. What joy greeted us when we arrived! Children crowded round to see what we had brought and they devoured the chocolate with great delight. We found that there was some food in the shops and markets but not in great quantities. A strong, crumbly cheese seemed to be available; this was mixed with herbs and rolled up in a kind of flat bread called *lavash* that was often eaten for breakfast. The lavash was sold in large rectangles in the markets – and people didn't seem to mind who had handled it! One or two restaurants were open, mostly frequented by businessmen. The thick menus would list a great variety of meals but, typical of the fSU, few were available.

The capital city, Yerevan, was built in a kind of basin with mountains surrounding it. Mt Ararat dominated the scene and glistened in the winter sunshine. It is believed that the remains of Noah's Ark are embedded in the ice at the top. In fact the Armenians, being the oldest Christian nation, take pride in believing that because of their close proximity to Mt Ararat they are the direct descendants of Noah. Although this famous mountain was part of the skyline from Yerevan, it was in fact in Turkey since that country had overrun much of Armenia in the early part of the twentieth century, massacring one and a half million Armenians and taking areas of their land.

As I assessed the situation I realized it was every bit as bad as I had been told. The winter was unbelievably cold and the one Russian-built nuclear power station (similar to the Chernobyl model) provided only one hour of electricity a day – its arrival being completely haphazard. Each part of the city had its hour; it could come in the day, the evening, or the middle of the night. This of course impacted on the electricity-dependent transport system. Vehicles would run for an hour and, when that hour was up, they would stop wherever they had reached and the poor passengers would tumble out. They were left to walk the rest of their journey because of course none of the link services were running either.

In people's homes everything was left switched on so that lights and appliances would start as soon as the electricity was available. "*Svet!*" (Light!) was the cry and suddenly everybody would jump to do the necessary chores before the current went off again. Everyone would work, even the children. Cooking and making hot drinks had to be done during this hour. It was a miserable situation. In addition, the tall apartment blocks were serviced by lifts and of course these were not working so everyone had to climb the stairs. It was difficult to imagine how the old people coped with this, or indeed anyone on the higher floors.

Hannah and I stayed in Ashot's apartment with his wife and two children. Next door lived his mother, father, and four sisters. It was very cold. As in all the other apartment blocks, anything made of wood such as stair rails and outer door frames had been stripped and the wood burned on the balcony to warm the apartment a little. All the trees in the streets and parks had been felled and burned. This gave the outside of the buildings a terrible appearance as soot marked the walls where the fires had been lit; of course there were no internal fireplaces in these communist-built high-rises.

Nothing of course had been repaired and so everywhere was shabby. This was a shame, for the centre of Yerevan had some attractive traditional architecture.

In an attempt to keep warm, Hannah and I wore seven layers of clothing and slept in three or four layers too, rolled in blankets and wrapped in thick duvets with a scarf around our heads. If we rinsed out any clothing, it froze on the cold radiators! As for washing ourselves, there was only cold water which had to be stored in the bath since a supply was only pumped up once every three days, and sometimes there was ice on it! I tried to be brave but afterwards it took two to three hours to rewarm my hands, so washing was minimal!

Wrapped up as best we could, we searched the town for the Jewish people Hannah had told me about – but they were gone; where, no one knew. Perhaps they had heeded my friend's exhortation to leave and go to Israel or maybe they were in Russia? We asked everyone we could, "Do you know any Jewish people?" but the answer was always the same: "No." We tried everything we knew and eventually after three days we were given a phone number. It was in this way we came to meet Villie and Reuben.

Villie was the leader of the Jewish community in Yerevan and Reuben was his cousin. They welcomed us to their home where Villie entertained us on the piano with Jewish songs. It was a real breakthrough and a breath of fresh air for us. We asked them to tell us about their situation but it was no better than that of anybody else: no one had helped them. We could tell that they were wondering if we would help, but they were also suspicious of our motives. Could we perhaps be missionaries?

We asked them about the possibilities of going to Israel. They said they couldn't go direct from Armenia but they could from Moscow. I knew it wasn't quite as simple as that and pointed out that the Moscow route might be difficult, suggesting that maybe there could be a plane from Yerevan after all.

"No." Villie was emphatic. "If we want to go, it has to be from Moscow."

We left, promising to send them some aid. However, the aid still had not arrived when the time came for us to leave Armenia.

We were disappointed but had to leave the joy of its arrival to the new Christian friends we had made. They were desperate for it, so we returned home to England hoping the delayed flight would eventually arrive.

Back in England my friend Hannah and I met again to discuss how things had gone. She said, "You know, Esther, we really need to take a whole planeload of aid. The boxes we've just sent won't go very far and there's such great need."

I knew she was right.

Before long she contacted me to tell me she had located a company that could arrange everything. The slight problem was that it would cost £40,000! We considered what such a step of faith meant. Still we couldn't shake the feeling that this was God's will; we had to go forward with this project. But what a price! Where was the money going to come from? Hannah and I didn't have any money to speak of. We lay face down on the floor and prayed.

That God was in it was proved very quickly because the answer came from a completely unexpected source. A member of the House of Lords, Baroness Cox, was at that time involved with an organization called Christian Solidarity Worldwide.[2] This group campaigns for religious freedom through advocacy and human rights. Hannah had been in contact with Baroness Cox because she was active in Armenia, and mentioned our plans to her. She immediately responded with enthusiasm and encouraged us to go ahead. Then incredibly she made a most generous offer of £12,000 towards the costs of the plane charter!

This was fantastic. Not only did we have the backing of someone in politically high places but we had a sizeable donation too. Only £28,000

---

2. Baroness Cox is now founder and CEO of HART (Humanitarian Aid Relief Trust), an organization supporting the oppressed and persecuted.

to go! Baroness Cox suggested we approach the UK government's Department for Overseas Aid and in fact she did so on our behalf.

Two days later we received a call that was mind-blowing. The government would pay for the plane! We couldn't understand why they were doing this but gave thanks to God that they were! When everything was explained, it turned out that the President of Armenia was coming to the UK for a state visit and it was important to show him that the UK was supporting his country. The government would take over the whole project and we could add any aid we wanted. Hallelujah! This was a case of God's perfect timing and we were greatly encouraged that we had heard from the Lord.

We learned that the aircraft would be taking off from Manston Airport in Kent so we realized we would need an aid collection point fairly close to it, probably somewhere in the north of that county. We spent some time in prayer and I received the word "Eltham." Hannah recognized it immediately as a small place near Bexley Heath, and what was more, she had a friend there. Along with the place name, I had also received in my mind a picture of a building: a single-storey structure, rectangular in shape, grey or beige in colour, with a pebble-dash exterior.

Hannah made contact with her friend, who agreed to help and suggested her church hall as a collection point. Once she had obtained permission from the minister, we drove across to see it. It was just as I had seen in my "picture" and the facilities were ideal for our purposes. We have an amazing God who confirms everything!

After arranging a date, we contacted all our friends and supporters. They brought (in a plethora of different vehicles) what seemed like tons and tons of clothing, shoes, and food of different kinds to the church hall. Here local believers helped to check, sort, and pack it all in huge cartons that had been made for transporting televisions. We also included some Christian literature.

People were so generous, such as the pensioners from a church in Southampton who hung a bag in their kitchen and put an item of food or toiletries in it each week. In this way they provided gifts for the elderly people of Yerevan. It was a marvellous and touching idea.

Sorting all the donations proved to be a huge task as the aid had to be classified according to the recipients, for example families, orphans, hospitals, and of course the Jewish people. Coloured tape identified each set of boxes to avoid confusion when the aid was unloaded in Yerevan. The hall was a hive of industry as people cleaned and polished shoes and sorted clothes; but it was wonderful too, laughing and fellowshipping with one another as we worked!

Hannah and I had wondered where we could stay overnight and thought to "camp" in the church hall. However, we needn't have worried; an amazing connection came to light that led to provision being made. Hannah's friend had met a lady she knew, called Margaret, in a supermarket in Bexley Heath. It turned out that Margaret and her husband had sponsored Ashot in Bible school in England. When she heard what we were doing she immediately wanted to help, and arranged accommodation and meals for us in her home. It was a wonderful example of Christian love, as she didn't even know us. We were so grateful. God's Hand was upon the whole project.

On the third day we took all the aid in a furniture van to Manston Airport where we met Baroness Cox and her team. The local media were there, plus a few dignitaries, and so photos were taken and speeches made. Afterwards someone took us by car to Whitstable where we stayed the night with a friend, June. She was thrilled to be doing something to help, and the next morning made us all breakfast before we drove to the airport.

When we saw that the plane we were using was a huge, old Russian military cargo plane that was designed to carry tanks, we realized we would never have been able to fill it ourselves. Our aid amounted to only two tons and the plane held fifty. Praise God for the government's intervention! The Lord knew exactly what we needed. On board were wheelchairs, artificial limbs and other medical equipment plus, incredibly, two ambulances! The eight of us going on the trip sat in the belly of the plane beside the aid. The pilots were Russian and very friendly; as we neared Armenia they invited Hannah and me to join them in the cockpit so we could get a glimpse of the snows of Mt Ararat sparkling in the dawn sunshine. How blessed we were!

On our arrival, Baroness Cox supervised the unloading of the aid, and our Armenian Christian friends came to the airport to help transport our part of it into the city. Some of the aid was of course destined for the Jewish community; one of the Christian brothers offered to transport this in an empty dustcart! Nevertheless it arrived safely – praise the Lord!

Baroness Cox and her team had to go on to Nagorno Karabakh, right into the main trouble spot, and asked me and Hannah to accompany them. This was amazing and we felt that it was God's will. It was our first flight in a helicopter and the views were incredible as we sailed over the mountains towards Stepanakert, the capital. Here, thanks to Baroness Cox, we were able to visit military hospitals, a command base near the front of the fighting, and their government headquarters – everywhere in fact that Baroness Cox went.

As fantastic as that was, it was an even greater joy to be free to pray with wounded soldiers in tent hospitals near the front and to comfort grieving relatives. Many of the soldiers were just young lads who had lost one or more limbs. They were amazingly cheerful despite their injuries and loved singing hymns to us.

In the town square we met survivors of previous massacres who told of appalling atrocities committed by their Muslim enemy: crimes too terrible to contemplate. And yet these gentle people seemed to be singularly lacking in hate, weeping as they related the horrors they had been through. We did our best to comfort them. We also asked if there was a Jewish community there, but were told there was none.

After two emotionally draining days of visiting these dear people in Nagorno Karabakh, we had a twelve-hour drive back into Armenia – through the mountains as the weather had become too unpredictable for any sort of flight.

When we got back, there was still some work to do distributing the unpacked aid, but it wasn't long before it had all found its way to the correct recipients. These included an orphanage where the children came running out to greet us. Food, clothing, teaching materials, two washing machines, and paraffin heaters were all received with great delight.

As there were still a few days left before our flight back home, we asked if we could see the area where the earthquake happened in 1988. It was a long drive over the mountains to the north of Yerevan to reach the zone. The epicentre had been at a place called Spitak, but the two towns of Leninaken and Kirovaken were both partially destroyed.

The main loss of life had occurred in the tall twenty-four-storey buildings which the Russians had been advised not to build. The tragic result of their folly was still before our eyes five years later. To say it was shocking was an understatement.

When the quake struck, the tall buildings had crumbled, each floor squashing the one beneath, and the evidence still lay in piles of rubble. Only the more traditional two- to three-storey Armenian houses had survived. Half the city of Leninaken had been affected and thousands had been killed. The survivors were still living without sanitation in makeshift huts (with snow dripping through the cracks), old containers, or even in the base of the collapsed buildings. They were crammed into any place that could be found. Dirt, dust, rubble, and mud characterized a scene which you could be forgiven for assuming had only just been created. Due to unemployment and the war situation, there was little hope of any change in the near future.

While walking around the town, we just "happened" to meet a beautiful young woman called Manik, who was from Ashot's congregation. She had been in Leninaken on the day of the quake, teaching at the music school. She told us that when the vibrations started and she realized what was happening, she had cried out to Jesus. She had been on the third floor of the building, which came down in one piece, with the result that she and her students were able to escape unhurt through a window! This was indeed a miracle as all the other floors had been flattened.

Manik knew that we wanted to find Jewish people and told us about the head of the music school. "He is so wonderful Jew," she said. "You must meet him." Unfortunately it was not to be that day, but we were grateful to hear about him and on a later trip we managed to locate him.

Through Manik we were able, on another trip, to bring aid to the needy of Leninaken.

We didn't visit the other affected town, Kirovaken, that day but apparently it was in a similar condition to Leninaken. Instead we drove on to Spitak, the epicentre. This town had been totally eradicated. It was impossible to believe that it had once been a town at all. We stood rooted to the spot, staring at the devastation which lay before us. It was eerily quiet. The solemn stillness shouted at me, like a silent scream, as I imagined what had happened: the cries of the injured and dying, the wailing of the bereaved. The grief was almost palpable. It was impossible to escape it.

On the day of our departure from Yerevan airport, we found, after we had checked in, that the flight had been delayed because someone had stolen the fuel for the plane!

The airport was cold. There was no food in the departure lounge and the hours started to tick by. Eventually the Red Cross came with a few blankets, a piece of bread, a small piece of cheese, and a hot cup of black tea for each person. We were there for twenty-two hours and felt somehow that we were in a place of identification with the Jewish people who often experience delays and long waits in the lands they wish to leave.

Finally, after a storm of protest by a BBC film crew who were on the same flight, enough fuel was found for our plane to depart.

As we started to board, we sensed an angelic presence. In fact it seemed that angels were all around the plane. It was truly a joy to be in the warmth of the cabin and to have a hot meal after waiting for so long.

Our hearts were full of thanksgiving for what had been accomplished. We knew that it wouldn't have happened without the Lord's timing and provision. We certainly couldn't have financed it ourselves!

CHAPTER 7

ALIYAH FROM ARMENIA

Do not fear, for I am with you;
I will bring your offspring from the east,
And gather you from the west.
I will say to the north, "Give them up!"
And to the south, "Do not hold them back."
Bring My sons from afar,
and My daughters from the ends of the earth.

(Isaiah 43:5–6)

In April, after we'd been back in England a short while, I telephoned Villie, the leader of the Jewish community in Armenia, to ask if he had received the aid we had brought and if it was in good condition. He was overwhelmed that we had kept our promise, for no one else had ever helped his people. His next words were mind-blowing. He asked, "Esther, do you think you could get a plane to take some of us to Israel?"

Without thinking I replied, "Yes, of course!" Then I wondered who was going to pay for this one. I mentioned it to Hannah.

"Of course," she said, "we have to do it!"

After a little search she found a company in Sussex with a reputation for daring rescues. It sounded perfect. We dressed in smart clothes to create the right impression (not that we had any money) and drove to the town where they had an office. We were soon chatting to three of their staff, one of whom was known as "Sport" because he loved exciting escapades!

"We want to take humanitarian aid into Armenia and then take some Jewish people from there to Israel," we said.

Sport and his colleagues were immediately interested and took us into what appeared to be an operations room with large screens on the wall. At the press of a button, up came a map of Europe and the Middle East. They plotted the route out to Yerevan in Armenia, then to Israel, and finally back to the UK. One of the big difficulties was the flight from Yerevan to Israel. It involved going over Muslim territories such as Iran and Syria whose governments didn't allow overflying en route to Israel. Also, flights from Armenia were not permitted over Turkish airspace. We would need to detour over Georgia and then in a big loop over Greece to get to Israel. Two "fingers" appeared on the screen and picked up the new path the plane would take. As the flight crossed each territory, the flyover tax appeared and added up. This was going to be costly. The total was £60,000!

Hannah and I both smiled at these gentlemen as if we were quite used to chartering planes at this kind of price! They wanted the first £20,000 within a month and the rest before we flew. We agreed an approximate date three months ahead and they told us they would arrange everything. This was reassuring; we didn't have to do anything else. Nothing else, that is, except pay! These men assumed we had the money but, as last time, neither of us had any at all! We shook hands and that was it. It was all very easy.

Outside, we stood on the pavement and looked at each other. What had we done? Into my head came the story in Mark chapter 11 of the time Jesus sent two disciples to fetch a colt. It was tied up, waiting just as He had said. Everything was pre-arranged. I related this to my friend and suddenly we both knew for certain that God would provide the money! If He had ordained this, as last time, He would provide. Rejoicing, we went and celebrated in a coffee shop.

Still feeling in awe, back at home we contacted our prayer partners to tell them about this new venture. I knew they would want to help but I had a sense that we were not to start raising funds for this plane. It was strange, but somehow I knew that God was going to pay for it His way and that we weren't to try and arrange it ourselves. This was truly faith-stretching. I had seen God provide money before but this was such a huge amount that it was tempting to start raising funds. However, I knew that if God was saying we must leave it to Him, then that was what we must do. This was a holy work and I was in awe and, in fact, a bit scared of touching it. Therefore when a supporter offered £60 towards the cost of the plane, I had to explain what I felt the Lord was saying. Thankfully she understood and agreed to put the money in the general fund.

We prayed of course, and as we felt the leading of the Holy Spirit we approached certain people to explain the project and the need. But we only approached those we felt God was directing us to. I was happy with this as I felt it was of the Lord. One of those I went to see was Gustav Scheller of Ebenezer Operation Exodus as I knew he would understand what we were doing. Patiently he listened to my story but, having just paid a large bill for his shipping contract taking Jewish people from Odessa to Haifa, he did not seem inclined to take on a new venture. He did agree, however, to pray about it.

In the meantime I approached one or two others, but more and more I felt in my heart that Gustav was God's man for this project. I kept him informed of our progress quite regularly, but whenever we spoke he informed me that the Lord had not told him to help. Even though he would have liked to, he knew, like us, that he must only do what God was telling him to and not act on what he thought were good ideas.

Hannah and I agreed that to move things forward I should go to

Armenia and gather the Jewish people together to tell them about the plane, while she prepared the aid and Bible-teaching materials. This seemed to be the right course of action as we both had experience in these respective areas, she with aid and me with the Jewish people.

More and more, I am fascinated with the way the Lord works. When He gives us something to do He does everything, and our role is just to cooperate in obedience. He arranges the right people, the right timing, the right situations – everything! It constantly amazes me. We just have to be available, ready, and listening, and then do what is in front of us. He promises to guide and He keeps His word. If He gives you something to do, wait on Him and believe that He will guide you.

I went back to Armenia, taking with me sixteen huge boxes on three trolleys. As it was humanitarian aid, I was allowed by British Midland Airways to take them cheaply; and they promised me that there would be someone at the airport in Paris (en route) to help me.

When I got to Paris the airline knew nothing of this. Furthermore they were not inclined to help. I loaded one trolley myself and felt I could push this, but I had three! Also the system for transit passengers at Charles De Gaulle airport at that time was far from straightforward. I stood there and prayed, "Lord, what am I to do? I need help." I even felt a bit tearful. What could I do with three trolleys to push?

After I had waited a short time, a stout lady in a dark uniform appeared from an office and looked at me. "You need help?"

I asked her if she was from British Midland Airways; she shook her head but indicated nevertheless that she would assist me. I positioned myself between the first two trolleys, this lady took her place between the second and third, and so we made progress, pushing and pulling until we reached the check-in desk for the Armenia flight. I looked round to line up the trolleys and thank her, but there was no one there! Once again I was left wondering if God had supernaturally sent one of His messengers to help me. I didn't know for sure, but He had certainly provided what I needed.

The plane took off and reached cruising height. I sat back, looking at the layer of cloud below as if we were flying just above a snow field. I thought about the help I'd had pushing the trolleys and I relaxed, confident that God would take care of all the details, not only of my trip but of the whole aliyah flight. Presently a warm Armenian sun caressed the wings of the plane, as though God was smiling on what we were doing, and the pilot brought us in safely to Yerevan airport.

Ashot and his friends met me with a van to collect the aid. I soon found myself again in Ashot's apartment being welcomed by his children who loved to help sort out the boxes.

Later on we met up with Villie who was delighted to see me and arranged a meeting of his people in a hall in the centre of town. I was given the opportunity, with Villie interpreting, to tell these dear people the news of the flight that would arrive and take them to Israel. From their point of view this must have sounded amazing: Gentiles bringing a plane to take them to Israel and it wasn't going to cost them anything? There were more than a few doubts and therefore lots of questions. Some, however, believed me and were keen to take this opportunity. A man called Sasha appointed himself to check everyone's documents and take their papers to the Consul to confirm their Jewish ethnicity. This was a great blessing as he and the other leaders of the community took over all these tasks while I had regular weekly meetings with the Jewish people to answer any questions they had, check their progress, and also encourage them.

Nearer the time of the flight, the Consul himself came twice to give out their visas for entering Israel, while we confirmed the situation about landing and take-off fees and check-in procedures with the airport authorities. We also arranged buses to the airport for the olim.

Villie and the other leaders of the local Jewish community booked a special dinner in a restaurant for the Consul and invited me too. Being of Russian culture, they performed many toasts with either wine or vodka. I declined the alcohol and had orange juice instead. This puzzled them, so I explained (with Villie translating) that I lose my sensitivity to the Holy Spirit if I drink alcohol, and as my contact with

Him is more precious to me than anything else, I prefer to stay away from it.

This testimony seemed to have a profound effect on those who were gathered and they began to ask about my beliefs. I think they thought I was Jewish. Villie pressed me emphatically, saying, "Go on, Esther; tell them about Yeshua" ("Jesus" in Hebrew).

I was surprised but decided to do so in a way I hoped they would understand. Standing up, I began to make a toast saying how special the Jews were as God's people and how He had chosen them to be a blessing to mankind.

I expected to be thrown out, but instead the Consul himself stood up and took over the translating as I told them, through my own testimony, the way of salvation. They loved it all and seemed to love me for telling them. It was incredible! Villie, the leader of the Jewish community who had told me to do this, afterwards confided in me that he had already accepted Yeshua as his Saviour. Praise the Lord for such an unexpected turn of events!

A Christian brother called Bagrat, who came to the Jewish meetings, informed me that his church, the Truth Church, had a "Mercy Team" whose members visited the Jewish community regularly. They helped the poor and elderly with household chores such as cleaning and washing, and also with shopping, in line with St Paul's declaration that "if the Gentiles have shared in their [the Jews'] spiritual things, they are indebted to minister to them also in material things" (Romans 15:27b). The congregation really understood this responsibility and also the need to pray for Israel. Their pastor had been to a Bible school in Moscow set up by the Swedish minister Ulf Ekman, who taught all his students about the significance of Israel. He had planted over 700 churches throughout the fSU and it later transpired that others from these churches came to our aid when we went on to help Jewish people in other cities. Indeed Bagrat became a very valuable asset, assisting me in finding other Jewish communities in Armenia and arranging transport when I needed it.

In the meantime back in England the deposit of £20,000 came in suddenly from a new charity that had just been registered. It was their first gift – hallelujah! Gifts for the general fund were arriving, as was aid which needed to be collected and sorted, but the large balance of £40,000 for the charter had yet to come in. I still felt that this money would come from Gustav Scheller but we had not heard from him.

"Why has Gustav not contacted us?" I enquired of the Lord one day. I had a strong impression that the Lord was saying, "I am testing his obedience." All we could do was trust and await God's timing.

The date arranged with the plane company for the flight seemed to be nearing fast. As it approached, Villie and I went to the airport in Yerevan to finalize arrangements with the airport authorities. Here we had a blessing. Because we were bringing in humanitarian aid, the landing and take-off fees would be waived (usually about $1,500) so we needed to pay only $500 for check-in procedures. Wonderful! I put $500 in an envelope and marked it clearly.

Next we ordered three buses to collect the olim (about ninety people) and arranged which routes they would take. We had of course hoped to fill the plane but so many of the Jewish people were doubtful about it all. Who could blame them? We were unknown to them, and leaving Armenia meant selling their property and trusting us completely. How many of us would do that?

It is hard to imagine the anxiety people go through in such circumstances unless one has been through it oneself. In addition, it was unusual for whole families to leave together. The usual pattern was for a family to send one or two of the stronger, healthier members to try it out, and then when good messages of the new land were received at home, the rest would follow.

The day before the flight arrived from England, we had a meeting for all the olim and immediately ran into a problem. Villie came rushing over to say that the Israelis, for some unknown reason, were refusing to let the plane land in their country. I told him not to worry. Despite this seeming setback, I felt confident that as the flight was God's work, God would sort this out. "Everything will be all right," I told Villie. He eyed me warily.

In faith we told the olim the timetable for the buses, and everyone went home. Some of these dear ones had travelled in from distant parts of the area and were already staying with friends. In spite of the news of this hiccup with the Israelis, there was an air of excitement which masked any concern about landing in Israel. I just could not believe we would be stopped.

However, the problems did not cease there. Hannah was in England organizing the payment for the plane. She still had no further money and the flight company wanted it before they would fly. The question was uppermost: "What do we do?" I could not help while in Armenia and in fact at the time didn't know what was happening in England. Hannah had tried everyone she knew in any case. She put the matter to Gustav once again and this time asked if we could borrow the money. Instead of turning us down, again he said he'd get his office team to pray. In fact we later found out that he sent out faxes to some intercessors as well, asking them to bring this matter before the Lord. Three people sent him the same Scripture: Luke 11:5–9 about the friend who came knocking at midnight and persisted in knocking.

"Well," he said, "Esther has been persistent in knocking. She is always sending me faxes, but yet God has not told me to give them the money."

At that moment a clock fell off the wall in one of the offices. The hands had stopped exactly at 12.00, and although it was midday everyone felt as though God was saying it was midnight – time was urgent! So Gustav agreed to lend the rest of the money – £40,000 – with the proviso that it was paid back within three months. How we rejoiced and praised the Lord when this news came through! (Actually I did not know all the details until the plane had landed.)

The next morning Villie came through with the same news that the

Israelis, for some reason, still would not let the plane land at Tel Aviv. I still did not believe it and shrugged it off. God would do a miracle. We had not come this far for everything to fail at the last moment.

We went to the airport; the olim began to arrive, each with 60 kilograms of luggage, and were directed to wait in a large hall. Villie and I were called to see the airport manager.

"Your flight is not coming," he said.

"What?" I replied. "Not coming – why not?"

Villie did all the talking and in the rapid verbal exchange forgot to translate it all to me. It seemed that the plane had not yet left the UK. We went over and over it with the manager, thinking there must be some mistake.

"No," he said, "it hasn't left yet; it is *not* coming. You must send the people home."

I would not believe it, and through Villie argued that there must be a mistake and that he had got it wrong: it must be on the way.

The man then said, "The plane must be lost."

In the work of God there is always opposition; things rarely go smoothly and we must press through, not giving way to difficulties the Enemy might throw at us. Finally the manager said he would have his staff search the airways again to see if the flight had left the UK, regardless of the earlier report. He put his hands on his desk to heave himself to his feet as he was a big man. Suddenly he noticed a fax lying on his desk. He picked it up and read it, saying incredulously that the plane had left the UK at 07.30, an hour after schedule. We were so relieved! This meant that, taking into account the four hours' flying time and the difference in time zones, it would be landing very soon!

The manager did not know what to say. Hallelujah! How we rejoiced in the fact that we serve a great and mighty God who never lets us down! The olim were waiting contentedly, eating snacks and drinking vodka, and we rushed down to tell them the good news.

In a very short time, the plane landed and we were allowed to go and greet the people on board. Only then did we get the details of why the Israelis were refusing to let the plane land. Apparently the official Israeli position was that there were no Jews left in Armenia so they didn't believe that the people we were bringing to Israel were real olim! To solve this problem Gustav, bless him, had used all his contacts in England, Russia, and Israel to reassure the Israelis that these were genuine olim. He had desperately wanted to come on the flight himself, but did not get any release from the Lord to do so and believed that the Lord wanted him to stay behind for some reason.

When Gustav found himself in the middle of this problem he realized why: he was the only one with the contacts to be able to sort it out. God is in everything and knows the plans He has for us.

In the end a delightful young Jewish woman from the Israeli Embassy in Britain came on the flight to check all the paperwork and ascertain whether those travelling were Jews or not. The Israelis were saying, "If they are Jews they can land in Israel; if not, they will have to stay in Armenia." Of course it didn't take long for this young woman to realize that all the olim were genuinely Jewish, and so we waited for them to be checked in.

In the meantime the aid that had arrived on the flight had to be unloaded and distributed among the Christian and Jewish communities. Those helpers who had come on the flight accompanied the aid into Yerevan, while we went inside to pay the $500 to the airport authority for the check-in procedure. I had been told that the landing and take-off fees had been waived so we went confidently with the special envelope that I had marked "$500" for this purpose. We hit another problem immediately.

The man who had assured me that the landing and take-off fees would be waived was not there. It was a different official, who knew nothing of the arrangement. He wanted the full fees and was adamant that we could not take off until we had paid them. In fact he was quite aggressive, and he and Villie got into quite an argument. Villie translated for me: it seemed this man wanted not $500 but $6,000 for the check-in, and another $3,000 for the landing and take-off fees.

This was preposterous. We didn't have such money and reiterated the arrangement we had made with the other official to pay $500, explaining that this was because we had brought in aid. In fact we pointed out that our country had brought in a lot of aid. But it was no use; this man would not let us leave until we had paid him $9,000. He said we had changed the arrangement by taking passengers out of the country and we could not leave until we had paid.

It appeared that we had hit a brick wall. We asked to see someone else and in fact spoke to many others, but it made no difference. We couldn't get around this demand for $9,000 and we simply didn't have such a sum.

In this situation we did the only thing anyone could do: we prayed. We prayed on and off all day and spent many hours in discussions with other officials. Eventually evening came and it started to get late. Exhausted after yet another fruitless conversation with an airport official, we went outside his office and prayed, asking the Lord what we should do.

Then clearly I heard the Lord say, "Get the money."

I turned to Hannah and exclaimed, "Get the money! God says 'Get the money' so it must be here!"

She looked at me quizzically.

I repeated to her, "The Lord has just spoken to me and said to get the money, so it must be here somewhere."

We went back to the big hall where all the Jewish people were waiting and found our pastor friend Ashot. Together we discussed the situation in the light of what the Lord had said so clearly. Hannah had $1,000 earmarked for aid. Ashot had $1,500 earmarked for his church building fund but he said we could borrow it and promptly drove home to fetch it. With the $500 I already had, we had $3,000 for landing and take-off fees. Would we be allowed to go now?

We took the money back to the airport manager's office and it was duly registered in his ledger.

"Can we go now?" we asked.

"No," he said. "You have to pay $6,000 more."

We felt desperate; no one had any more money.

Hannah went back to the Jewish people to reassure them while I went back into the office we had just left. The man there spoke English so I didn't need an interpreter. I told him again that we simply did not have the money he was asking for.

An idea came to me. I suggested to him that he keep me there (a bit like a hostage) and let the Jewish people go to Israel. "After all," I said, "our friends will send the money to you quickly and that will solve the problem."

He would have none of this. "Absolutely not," was his response.

I guess I was not worth £6,000. I felt a bit silly but it had been worth a try.

Outside his room I stood in a corner to pray. An emptiness born of desperation churned in the pit of my stomach. I had truly come to the end of my own resources. We had tried everything and there was nothing more we could personally do.

It was late and the airport was dark because there was no electricity on. It felt as if the Enemy was aiming arrows at me. Downstairs, Villie had wanted to tell everyone to go home and we had told him, "No, absolutely not; God has the answer."

Now what could I do? I had no answer to encourage him. I was empty of all solutions to this problem. We had a hall full of people, a bill of $6,000, and nothing I could think of would get us out of this nightmare.

The darkness of the stairwell seemed to reflect the hopelessness of the situation and I cried out to the Lord: "Oh God, have we been two foolish women acting out of our own ideas? Was all this our own plan? We owe another $6,000 and we do not have the money. What is the answer? Help us, Lord."

Immediately the Lord spoke to me.

"Go to the pilots," He said.

"Go to the pilots? Go to the pilots?" I repeated to myself as I raced down to the hall where the olim were waiting patiently. Many were asleep, some stretched out on luggage, others on what few seats there were, still others on the floor. They were used to this kind of situation in the communist era – endless queuing, waiting, coping with problems – and it seemed that nothing had changed. They were such patient, uncomplaining, stalwart people.

I found Hannah. "We have to go to the pilots," I blurted out to her. "God said so."

The airport was now in complete darkness because of the electricity blackout. Somehow Hannah and I found our way out to the apron where planes were standing in the loneliness of inactivity. There were no security personnel around and no one stopped us. We tried to recognize our plane. Suddenly we saw a torch light come on in one of the planes and we went to check it out. It was ours! The crew of three pilots and three stewardesses had been waiting, wondering what the delay was and not knowing what to do. We explained the situation.

"We need another $6,000," I told them, "otherwise we won't be allowed to take off. And we don't have any more money."

"What?" said the Captain in disbelief. "Did you say $6,000?"

He put his hand inside his blazer pocket and pulled out a big wad of notes tied with an elastic band.

"Here," he said. "I think you'll find this is $6,000. Take it and let's leave."

We just stared at him, dumbfounded. Later he told us how he happened to have the money with him. As well as being one of the pilots, he was also a director of the company. He had been at home, dressing, putting on his jacket before coming to the airport, and had noticed the pile of notes lying nearby, which he had not had time to bank. For some inexplicable reason he had an urgent feeling to put the money in his pocket rather than leave it at home. This made no sense to him as he knew he wouldn't have any spare time to find a bank or go shopping. But the feeling was so strong he grabbed the notes and stuffed them in his pocket. He wasn't even a believer and didn't know why he felt the urge to take them; he just gave in to the feeling. God knew why and had arranged everything! How we praised God!

Elated, we ran back into the airport to find the official and pay the money quickly. We handed the money over. It was almost midnight by now.

"Can we go now?" we asked.

"No," he said, "not until the flight from Paris has landed and taken off again. That will be in two to three hours."

It seemed the Enemy was throwing every spanner he could find into the works to stop or hinder our olim from going to Israel. We waited an extra hour for the Paris flight to come and go as it was delayed, and then we went again to ask if our plane could take off. This time we were ushered into another room where more officials wanted to ask questions. One of our pilots came too, but we didn't know why. Later we found out that he knew what pressure we were being put under and wanted to help us.

The officials asked us, "Who gave you permission to take our citizens out of our country?"

For a moment we were stunned. What sort of question was this? What did they mean?

Without request our helper stepped in and pointed out that our passengers were leaving of their own free will and had the Armenian government's permission to leave and the Israeli government's permission to enter Israel. So what was the problem?

This took the officials by surprise but they were not so easily put down. They said that we had brought a foreign plane onto their soil and had not used Armenian Airlines. And they wanted to know how much each person had paid for his or her ticket.

"Nothing," we answered. "Their tickets are free."

"Free! Free – how can they be free? What do you mean?"

Our answer really floored them. My friend Hannah spoke up: "It's humanitarian aid."

"Humanitarian aid? Taking Jews to Israel is humanitarian aid?"

We explained that the olim could not afford to pay anything to go to Israel so their flight had been paid for by voluntary donations from Christians in the UK who believed it was right to assist them.

One of the officials again chimed in: "You mean their tickets are free?" as if this point had not been made clear enough already.

"Yes," we replied, "but they don't actually have tickets."

"No tickets! No tickets – how can this be?" one of them exclaimed.

They had never heard of such a thing. The full implication of what we were saying now seemed to be gradually sinking in, much like a coin thrown into the sea, swaying backwards and forwards on its descent to the bottom.

Eventually they gave in and accepted what we were saying. It became apparent that what these men were up to was another opportunity to extort money from us. No doubt they had seen that when we were under pressure we could come up with thousands of dollars, so they thought they would try it again. They had wanted a percentage of the value of each person's ticket, and because the tickets were free that wasn't going to happen. They were stumped. Hallelujah!

However, not to be outdone, they tried something else. They said that their staff were paid to process only passengers of Armenian Airlines, not ours, and we would have to pay extra for this.

What next? we wondered.

After negotiating with the authorities, it was agreed that we would pay $3 for each passenger. This didn't seem so bad compared with the costs we had faced before, and by asking around we eventually got the money together as we only had sixty-four passengers in total. This was quite remarkable as the crowd in the airport numbered many more than this, and it became apparent that a large number were relatives saying farewell. This wasn't a problem. Of more concern was that there were others hoping to get a ride to Israel just to visit family. Although we had sympathy for this and would willingly have let them go on the plane, the lady from the embassy thought it prudent to exclude the visitors in case the Israelis refused to let them into the country. All through the proceedings, she turned out to be a marvellous support. As it turned out, it would have been all right for them to go; but we didn't know that then.

At last we were given the go-ahead and our dear, patient passengers gathered up their belongings and went through check-in. Thankfully none of the airport officials harassed them. Perhaps they were sympathetic after all the trouble there had been.

At this point Hannah and I had to say farewell to the olim as we were not going with them to Israel. We went out on a balcony to watch them board the plane. There it was – our beautiful plane, white with a red stripe, and the word "Omega" emblazoned on its side. Jesus is called "the Alpha and the Omega, the first and the last, the beginning and the end" (Revelation 22:13). We were thrilled; it was God's plane carrying His dear ones home to the Promised Land.

We watched as it set off down the runway with the pilot, Sport, at the controls. It gathered speed until at last it zipped into the air, its nose pointing skyward as if toward heaven. As it climbed higher we saw an amazing thing: a huge angel blowing a trumpet in front of the plane! It was clear – the battle had been won. Hannah and I looked at each other and dissolved into tears, hugging each other. The flight that the Enemy had tried so hard to stop so many times was on its way, and we knew without any shadow of doubt that it was all God's doing. The aliyah highway from Armenia had opened!

When we calculated all the time at the airport, we realized that the poor olim had spent twenty-two hours there without a word of complaint – the exact time we had been delayed previously.

We headed back to Ashot's house for some much-needed rest. In his living room we gathered to pray and think. The flight had taken place, the plane company had been paid by loans, but we still had a debt of $99,000 (£66,000)! It was easy to imagine that because the flight had left, everyone would rejoice and forget that we owed all this money. However, for me and Hannah it loomed very large in our minds. We had no idea where the money was coming from.

As we prayed I had a picture of a bill with "PAID IN FULL" written across it. I told this to the others who were gathered there. Suddenly the fax machine started buzzing. It was a message from Gustav. He had received another Scripture, Luke 6:30, this time from his wife, Elsa, to the effect that he shouldn't ask for repayment of the sum he had loaned. He was relieved: God had given him instruction at last to pay for the olim flight from Armenia to Israel. How we praised the Lord! This left only the $6,000 borrowed from the pilot and another $3,000 borrowed from various others such as Ashot, for different expenses. The debt of $3,000 was covered fairly quickly by donations. Praise the Lord!

We then went to the office of the plane company to find out exactly what we owed as we expected there would be extra charges. After all, there had been delays, and their stewardesses and pilots had worked longer hours than they were contracted for. We went over the whole story and afterwards the director, Mr Mack, smiled and said we didn't owe them anything more. It had all been covered. "You owe us nothing," he said.

"What about your own $6,000 that you lent us?" I asked.

"No, you owe us nothing; it's all covered," he repeated.

We were dumbfounded. God had surely directed us to this man, knowing he would be there for us in our hour of need, and he wasn't even a believer!

Our hearts were full of praise and thanksgiving to God and also gratitude to these men who had given us and God's precious Jewish people so much. Hallelujah! They had been committed to the flight 100% as had we. However, we were also under no illusion about who had initiated and completed the project. It was God and God alone. We had just been obedient and followed His direction as we faced all the problems we encountered on the way.

It is quite normal, when ministering in any way to Jewish people, to face spiritual opposition. This is because Satan is constantly trying to thwart God's purposes for Israel. If he could destroy Israel he could prove God a liar because God has committed Himself to Israel and her future. His covenant with her is eternal. And so Satan does everything he can to disrupt and destroy whatever is done on behalf of the Jewish people. It was because of this, then, that after our wonderful flight from Armenia, I was summoned to Jerusalem to face a very angry man indeed!

CHAPTER 8

MORE ALIYAH
FROM ARMENIA

A gentle answer turns away wrath.

(Proverbs 15:1a)

The man in the Jewish Agency in Israel responsible for aliyah from the whole of the fSU was very angry indeed and demanding to see me. This unsettling news had been communicated to me by Gustav Scheller who had financed the flight from Armenia to Israel. I therefore prepared myself, and after a short rest in the UK went to Jerusalem and made an appointment to see him.

Armed with my rather large King James Bible I went to see Mr "Y," who greeted me politely if not cordially. But upon seeing my Bible he thumped his desk, stood up, and shouted, "Don't start quoting that book at me! I've heard it all from Mr Scheller. You've caused me a lot of trouble bringing a British plane into Armenia!"

I sat down, despite the lack of invitation, looked at him, and wondered why he was so angry. I waited quietly.

He continued, "You know there is a war on. We are trying to get the Jewish people out of Baku [in Azerbaijan]. They let us take the women and children but not the men – they want them for 'army fodder' and won't let them go. Now you've taken our people out of Armenia, which is their enemy, and used a British plane too. Don't you realize what a sensation this has caused? They won't let me take their Jews out now for sure – none of them – and it's your fault!" He sat down heavily, still glaring at me.

I somehow failed to see why the Azeris should mind if Jewish people left Armenia but I didn't say so. In spite of this verbal attack I felt strangely calm and at peace, knowing we had obeyed the Lord in bringing the Jews out. In a controlled manner I posed the question of what he himself intended to do for the Jews of Armenia – after all, they were also part of a war. He said that as far as he knew there were none left! I therefore surprised him when I told him there was an active Jewish community in Yerevan of around 300 people.

He calmed down somewhat and asked about their living conditions and how we had found them. Even then he implied that we should not be helping them to leave. This was too much and so I asked him again what he and his staff intended to do for them. "After all," I continued, "you haven't even got an office there or anyone to represent you."

What followed was completely unexpected, for he challenged me and said, "You get me forty Jews and I'll get you a plane."

"Done!" I replied. (I love a challenge.)

We shook hands on the "deal" and parted more amicably than we had met, his card and contact details in my hand.

Very soon I returned to Yerevan, this time alone as Hannah wasn't able to come. I thought I would need to rent a small room in the centre of town so, knowing the great shortage of food, my friends packed me two large cartons of tins and jars. I also took with me several boxes of aid on two trolleys.

Dear Ashot and his friends met me, and he would not hear of my renting a room so I stayed with him and his dear family once more.

One of his friends, Samuel, offered to drive me everywhere if I could buy a battery for his car and pay him for his petrol and assistance. This was a great help and everything was agreed.

It was wonderful that so many supporters had been touched by the situation in Armenia and had sent in funds. This money enabled me to action so much help for the community in Yerevan, and sharing it with Ashot and his band of helpers made a real, positive impact on their suffering. I learned that when God guides He provides, and I made it a rule not to ask for money, ever. I make my petitions only to the Lord and He puts His desires on the hearts of the people; over the years they have given very generously and still do. God always provides for need, not greed, and He has never let me down.

After contacting Villie, I discovered that Sasha had now been appointed by Mr Y in Israel to be the Jewish Agency's representative in Yerevan. It seemed that our meeting had had an impact and Mr Y had wasted no time! However, before we could arrange a flight, we needed to find Jewish people who were ready to leave.

During the last trip, Hannah and I had visited the two cities of Leninaken and Kirovaken. These places had been badly damaged by the 1988 earthquake and we had heard that there were some Jewish people there.

In Leninaken we met one family who lived in a dark, damp basement of a block of flats that now crumbled around them. Water was only available by accessing an uneven rock-strewn path, and heating and lighting were supplied for only an hour a day, as in Yerevan; otherwise it was candles or darkness and cold. The family had four grown-up children – a married daughter who lived abroad somewhere, a son called Andrei who had cerebral palsy, able only to move one arm, and another son and daughter.

The mother, Rosa, had fallen on the ice in winter while getting water and had broken her hip. They had no money for hospital treatment so she had stayed in bed until the hip began to heal. Now she hobbled about, using a stick.

The father, Edvard, was a talented musician and had taught in the music school. All the family had once tried to emigrate to Israel but without success and had unfortunately given up. Edvard was a lovely, gracious man who had been through terrible suffering. He told us how during World War Two he had been buried alive under a pile of bodies, victims of a gas attack. Instead of treating him with compassion, the Russians decided that because he had survived he was a traitor, and had imprisoned him for fourteen years! But far from becoming bitter, he had found grace to overcome his suffering and had gone on with life. He was quite inspiring.

The family made us a meal in spite of their difficult circumstances: a sort of stew made from vegetables and served with bread. How humbling it was for us as we wondered what we would have done in their situation. We determined in our hearts that there had to be a way for us to help them. We couldn't leave them to live like this. There had to be a solution.

As I travelled about, I remembered others from the last trip who needed to be contacted. There had been a couple outside one of the meetings in Yerevan whom we had found weeping. They had explained they were anxious about their family over in Nagorno Karabakh who were desperate to make aliyah but could not get out because of the trouble there. Plus, their situation was made worse by the fact that they had no passports. This news had come despite our being told there were no Jews left in Nagorno Karabakh. They then told us there were in fact two families there, both wanting to leave. We had made a promise to help them if we could, giving them hugs of encouragement.

Then there was Villie's friend in Stepanakert. After the last flight, we had gone by helicopter back into Nagorno Karabakh and visited this family. Like Villie, the father was a musician and had arranged for us to meet with them plus the other family. Thankfully they had documents to prove their Jewish ethnicity but were facing problems being allowed to leave the country.

We also found out that there were several women in Nagorno Karabakh who were from Ukrainian families that had managed to escape there when the Nazis overran Ukraine. They had such harrowing stories, typical of Jewish families on the run from persecution. It was not surprising they were keen to go to Israel if there was any chance. Unfortunately they had no documents, and to make aliyah the correct papers have to be in place. They all wanted to leave so we promised to see what could be done.

As I remembered all these dear ones whom I had met on the previous trip, I recalled the journey back over the Shushi Mountains. We flew in a larger helicopter for the return trip because there were two badly wounded soldiers on stretchers in the mid section. They were critically injured and were being transported along with their relatives and the medical staff to a hospital. The pilots were not at all certain that they had enough fuel to make the trip but were determined to try for the sake of the two injured soldiers. Hannah and I had been squeezed in, and sat on two wooden boxes at the back. What an opportunity to pray! We prayed and prayed, against demonic spirits of death that might claim the lives of these soldiers, against the poor visibility because of thick cloud, and against the shortage of fuel that could realistically claim all our lives. God was covering everything, however, and – to His glory – once we were safely over the mountains we landed in a field where the pilots were able to refuel.

What a mighty God we serve! I thought as I mused on all these things.

Bringing my thoughts back to the present time, I knew I had to try and get these people out along with the others in Yerevan who wanted to leave. I decided to arrange some meetings each Friday at 3.00 p.m. in a hall in the centre of town. By the numbers of people that attended I knew that confidence was growing in what we were doing. People had seen relatives arrive safely in Israel, and good reports were coming back which encouraged them. Sasha in his new role of Jewish Agency representative started to record names and prepare the papers that would be needed.

In the meantime Bagrat, from the Truth Church, arranged to take me on a visit to Kirovaken to visit Jewish people who were known to them through their "Mercy Team" whose members helped the elderly with shopping and household chores. Through this work, the church came into contact with people who might not have attended the community activities. I got my fishing tackle ready!

In Jeremiah 16:16 the prophet talks about a time when God will send for fishermen to catch the Jews, and I used to tell people that whenever I look for Jewish people I take my fishing tackle with me. This used to produce some questions about nets and rods and bait! In fact my "tackle" was various forms of information about life in Israel but most effectively the Word of God. I used it to show Jewish people that God loved them and was calling them back from all around the world to the Land that He gave them. As His people they had been disobedient and judged, but now through the establishment of the State of Israel He was restoring them to the Land as part of His prophetic purposes and to show the world that He keeps His promises.

When we found Jewish people we would give them several items: an illustrated leaflet we'd made that listed Scripture verses related to the ingathering; photographs showing the landscape, housing, and shops in Israel; audio cassettes of Israeli music; videos featuring people who had already made aliyah; and information about the programme of help that the Israeli government provided. This package of assistance is called an "absorption basket" and includes finance, initial accommodation, schools for children, and Hebrew classes – in fact everything immigrants need for their first year in Israel. It's quite remarkable.

The olim loved all these things but without a doubt the Scripture verses seemed to touch their hearts the most. They said so quite often, and this confirmed what the Bible says about itself:

The Word of God is quick, and powerful, and sharper than any two-edged sword . . .

(Hebrews 4:12 KJV)

In Kirovaken, Villie had arranged for all the Jewish people to assemble together to meet me. Bagrat had come with me, and Samuel had driven the hour's journey through the mountains to get there. The meeting was in a room that was part of the remains of an apartment block that had been damaged in the earthquake. The floor was sloping and the windows also were slanted – it looked really unsafe. I was shocked to discover that this dangerous place was the permanent home of one family. There was no light or heat except for the usual one-hour period as in Yerevan. The people appeared grubby and the men unshaven, which was hardly surprising since the only water available was from a standpipe outside – and that water was cold.

We gave the people the usual "fishing gear," but of course they had no means of either listening to the music cassettes or watching the videos. They looked at the brochures containing the photos and we read them the pertinent Scripture verses.

"Oh," they said, "Israel is just a dream – a vision, far away. We could never go there. It's only a dream."

They were adamant that they would not go. It was not for them, they said. "Things will change here," they claimed. Their present situation was so bad they could not even make us a cup of tea and yet incredibly they would not consider going to Israel! There was nothing we could do.

On the way back we called at Leninaken to visit the family who had a son with cerebral palsy. Bless them, they were so cheerful. We discovered that the son could play chess by signalling his move with a thumb which his brother could interpret! His father, Edvard, played his violin for us and we saw how talented he was with the instrument.

We longed to help them, so Bagrat took all their details along with their documents. We determined that we would try our hardest to get them to Israel even though they had been refused before. The sticking point, it seemed, had been that a past relative in Poland had been registered as Catholic, probably to escape persecution. The Consul had been suspicious that they might really be Christians trying to get out of Armenia and not really Jewish at all; so he had refused their application. They had been devastated and too discouraged to try again. We knew that God could open doors that no one could shut (Revelation 3:8) and so we decided to pray!

Meanwhile Bagrat and Villie had arranged for us to go to Nagorno Karabakh again, this time in a bus over the mountains rather than by helicopter! We took some boxes of clothing for the Jewish people there and, despite the possibility of problems at the border, were waved through without a hitch. This was because the border guards amazingly recognized me from the previous visit with Baroness Cox, and shouted, "Baronessa Cox! Baronessa Cox!" I felt a little like royalty and was made very welcome.

One of the Jewish ladies, Rosa, had assembled everyone together and we shared out the hand-knitted garments that we had brought with us. The people were overwhelmed to think that others cared about them so much. Rosa was very well organized and had a list of all their names and phone numbers. The main problem, and this was serious, was that several of them had no documents to prove that they were Jewish. Their parents had fled there ahead of the Nazis and had destroyed any papers they possessed which revealed their Jewish roots. Without documents it is nigh impossible to make aliyah. Rosa's family, plus one other, did have the papers to prove they were Jewish but unfortunately still could not leave because they did not have passports. In fact, until the dispute over Nagorno Karabakh was finally settled, they were stateless.

We talked with them at length, encouraging them not to give up and telling them that God had a way to get them out. We gave them the Scripture verses and other "fishing tackle," and left with our promise that we would not abandon them and would be back.

Sasha, the Jewish Agency representative, had collected the papers of the many potential olim he had on his list, and took the documents to Moscow to see the Israeli Consul. In time the Consul came to Yerevan, where over a period of three days he was to interview each applicant. We had been told that this man was new to the job and very strict.

Many people were gathered outside the hall, waiting for his car to arrive. Three or four ladies were crying and told me they had already been refused.

"Please, please speak to him for us," they begged me.

I said I would try and so stood at the edge of the kerb to catch the Consul as he got out of his car. This was my only chance; I threw a prayer skywards and stepped into his path. I told him of these ladies and their cry for help, but he was not moved. However, he did suggest I should sit next to him as he interviewed the people.

"Then you'll get an idea of the problems I have," he retorted. He stared at me for half a second and said, "Look, if I allow all these women into Israel and they are not Jews, I'll get into a great deal of trouble."

The first person came and handed in his papers. The Consul took one look at them and threw them back at the man, saying, "Get out of here; don't try bringing me false papers." The man left without a word. Thankfully most of the other applicants had paperwork which satisfied his requirements.

Then it was the turn of one of the ladies whom I'd spoken to him about. She had a sweet face and a gentle demeanour. She had no papers because she had fled from Azerbaijan, leaving everything behind to seek safety with relatives in Armenia. She had photos of herself attending a Jewish school and could speak Yiddish. One would have thought this would have impressed the Consul, but no. I, however, was very impressed; you could see from the photos that she was telling the truth, and I told him so.

Pointing at the photograph, I said, "She's holding a Jewish textbook; she's wearing a garment with a Jewish symbol on it; she can speak Yiddish and even sing Yiddish songs. You have to let her go!"

The Consul's problem was that if she was indeed Jewish then he would have to consider allowing eight other members of her family to go too.

"But you can see that she's Jewish," I went on. "It's clear." I kept pressing the point home.

With a big sigh he agreed to get his Moscow office to check the archives in Baku to verify her Jewish ethnicity. If what she was saying was true, she could go to Israel.

I had to leave it at that. Unfortunately he would not consider the other ladies, and I had to leave them to source their own paperwork and try again another time.

Later on, all those who had been approved got their visas stamped in their passports and the flight was arranged – Mr Y had fulfilled his promise that if I got him forty Jews he would get me a plane. We had actually doubled it: eighty olim left for Israel in September in time for the Feast of Tabernacles. It was a great time to make aliyah.

> *Has He said, and will He not do it?*
> *Or has He spoken, and will He not make it good?*
>
> (Numbers 23:19b)

Back in the UK I went down to Bournemouth to see Gustav Scheller and his team. He wanted to go to Armenia himself and said that if the Jewish Agency would set up another flight, Ebenezer Operation Exodus would pay for it.

"A third flight!" I was really excited.

"Will you go and get the people ready?" he asked. I was thrilled. The plan was that I would go out first and gather the Jewish people together as before. Gustav and Elsa would come out later and meet the olim themselves just before the aliyah flight left.

Once again I obtained a visa for the usual six weeks and packed my warmest clothes, expecting to be back in the UK by the end of November. I also took several boxes of aid as before and some finance to help the people who looked after me in Armenia.

The Lord never failed to provide the money that was needed for everything, whether it was aid for the people or my own airfares and expenses. I had none of my own to speak of and it was wonderful to see how funds came in on time when the need was there. So many obedient and faithful people who were praying for me heard from the Lord and sent money in, sometimes in large amounts and sometimes in small amounts, but it was all from God. I might have been the one out in the "field" but their role was just as important, for without it I couldn't have done my part. Winston Churchill in one of his speeches once quoted John Milton about the valuable role each person played during the Second World War. He said, "They also serve who only stand and wait." I would change that and say rather, "They also serve who only stand and pray."

While in England, I went around to the various groups that prayed for me, sharing what was happening, as everyone was excited about the flights. I was very tired and all the time had a pain down my right arm which had not responded to prayer. There was just one week remaining before I was due to leave for Armenia, when a rash appeared all down my arm and across my chest: small spots in circles. Pains like red-hot knives jabbed at me at regular intervals.

Passing a doctor's surgery that day, I heard the Lord say, "Go in there." I went in and showed the GP the rash.

"Madam," he said, "you have a classic case of shingles!"

He then told me that I must keep warm and rest; the problem would probably last about six months and be very painful. He prescribed some strong painkillers and told me to come back when I needed more.

All the time I was with the doctor, I was saying under my breath, "I'm not going to have this," and was thinking about the trip ahead of me. Anyway, I collected the prescription and returned to where I was staying. I told no one except Hannah on the telephone. She prayed, and my head cleared a little so that I felt better.

Lying on the floor, I put it to the Lord. Either He did not want me to go to Armenia and organize this flight, in which case He had allowed me to have the shingles, or it was Satan trying to stop me from going. To keep warm in an Armenian winter was as impossible as it was to rest while doing this work.

I felt the Lord impress on my heart, "Are you not the person trained to do this job? Have I not led you thus far? Is it not My plan for your life to help My Jewish people go home to Israel?"

I could only answer, "Yes, Lord." Then I asked Him to heal me and said that even if He didn't, I would still go because I knew now that it was His will.

At this point the phone rang. It was a friend calling to tell me about three big meetings that weekend in the city. It turned out that the third was to be led by a couple from the London Healing Mission. Immediately I knew that this was of God and that I should go.

I went to the meeting and responded to the invitation for prayer. The leader prayed for me and instantly I was healed: no more red-hot knives, nothing! I was dancing for joy and so were my friends when I told them. I knew that when God is in something, the results come and He works the miracles needed. I still had the painkillers and took them to Armenia for elderly folk who had arthritis – they were not wasted. Hallelujah – what a mighty God we serve!

The week passed quickly and after what was becoming a familiar flight from the UK, Ashot met me at the airport in Yerevan; soon I was welcomed back into his home by his wonderful wife and children. A call came in from England: it was Gustav to tell me that he was sending a young lady from Ebenezer to Armenia. There was nothing specific for her to do in Ebenezer at that time, so he thought it would be good to send her to me and she could help me and learn about the work. I readily agreed.

A few days later we were at the airport welcoming a very attractive young lady from the Czech Republic called Vlasta. She was a breath of fresh air for us, with her wonderful sense of humour and infectious laugh. She eagerly participated in everything we did.

I contacted Villie to see how things were going, but he was strangely reserved.

"What's wrong?" I asked him.

He replied that the Jewish Agency had given them instructions that they must not work with me any more. They could do everything themselves and therefore further involvement with Christians was unnecessary. I was stunned. I reasoned with him and he agreed that we had worked well together but what could he do about his orders? Orders were orders.

When Gustav and Elsa arrived, I explained the unexpected turn of events. They couldn't even meet the Jewish community in Yerevan. All we could do was pray and wait.

In the meantime we went to Leninaken and Kirovaken with Bagrat, who had arranged for us to meet with the community there. To our great joy and amazement the Jews who had previously said that going to Israel was just a dream, and not to be taken seriously, had been busy getting their papers in order. They had read the Scripture verses we had left and it seemed that the Lord had touched their hearts. All of them were planning to make aliyah except for one couple who decided to stay as the husband had a good job. What an amazing turnaround and what a cause for thanksgiving – God had changed their minds! We were so excited and indeed so were they. We told them about the imminent flight and this spurred them on to take their papers to the Consul.

Despite the orders that Villie and Sasha should not work with us, we soon saw that God had other plans and was answering our prayers about the situation. Bagrat and I had been visiting those Jews whom we knew, encouraging them to go to Israel. Word of this found its way to Villie and Sasha who had been obediently and steadfastly following their orders and ignoring our enquiries. However, it wasn't long before the Jewish community themselves started to ask for us and we were invited back to the planning meetings; I was even greeted with two bunches of roses. The Lord had done it!

Everything went well. The Consul came twice, once to interview people and examine their papers, and once to stamp the visas in their passports. The plane was expected by late November before the onset of really bad winter weather: snow, fog, and ice. So we waited.

At times when we were not visiting Jewish people or busy with preparations, I would teach Ashot's congregation some English – just phrases, but it was great fun and the source of much laughter. As the Scripture says, "A joyful heart is good medicine" (Proverbs 17:22) and it cheered us up no end. I thought I must have been a poor teacher when I heard phrases like "I am married and have one husband," or "I cleaned my tooth," or "I ironed my hair," but everyone enjoyed themselves.

Autumn was now moving fast into winter. The summer-visiting birds had long since left and one could feel the cold deepening its grip, especially in the tall Soviet-built apartment blocks with little heating. We had brought with us from England several small electric heaters for Ashot, which meant that for one hour each day we had a little more heat. With the help of the old oil stove which we could huddle round, and candles to give some meagre light, we managed.

Amazingly it became possible to buy bottles of camping gas, and as Hannah on a previous occasion had brought over a little stove with two gas rings we were able to make hot drinks and even cook small meals – bliss! We really thanked the Lord for this.

I had a hot-water bottle for night time which, if kept in its cover all night, was still a little warm in the morning; the contents could then be poured into a plastic bowl and used for my morning wash. Compared with washing in ice-cold water it was luxury. One becomes very enterprising when the need arises.

Actually, getting washed became a story in itself. Ashot's family possessed an electric water heater rather like the small coils we used for making tea. This one was about 25 centimetres long, and when the hour's electricity was running (which could be at any time of the day or night) they used it to heat a big, deep pail of water. The members of Ashot's own family, plus his mother and sisters next door and I, amounted to ten people in all. So we each took a turn to use this water once in ten days to have a "shower." Of course, it wasn't really a shower. One had to stand in a baby bath and pour the water over oneself with a jug, but it was great to have a wash. Needless to say, with the splashing and the steam condensing and running down the walls, the floor got rather damp. Then when the hour's electricity was over, the winter temperature kicked in and the water on the floor and walls froze! Anything on the floor you wanted to keep dry had to have a plastic bag underneath it; otherwise it got wet from the melting ice when the hour's electricity started.

Washing clothes was an even greater trial. My small things I did in the warm water from my hot-water bottle after I'd had my morning wash, then hung them over the radiator in my room. They dried eventually, but this often entailed taking them to bed with me to finish them off. The family did have a washing machine but had to leave it on all the time so that over several days of one-hour-a-day electricity the machine would complete its cycle. The bigger clothes would then be hung outside whatever the weather; over several days of freezing and thawing and hanging in the wind, they would finally get dry. No one changed clothes very often because of this – maybe once a week, rather like when I was a child: a bath on Saturday and clean clothes on Sunday.

Sleeping at night entailed donning several layers of clothing which were exchanged in the morning for another set. It is difficult for people in centrally heated Western homes to appreciate what it's like living under these conditions. The Armenian Christians did not have an easy life, and what little of this world's goods they did have they were willing to share with others. They were a real testimony to Christian love and selflessness.

Bagrat brought us some news. Villie had confided in him that while I had been in England, two ladies from Nagorno Karabakh had come by bus to Yerevan for "shopping" – a trip allowed by the authorities. Sasha had checked their papers as he was the Jewish Agency representative and assured them that everything was fine and they could go to Israel. One of the ladies, Rosa, had excitedly phoned home to her husband saying, "We can go! We can go!" He was immediately arrested. The other lady, Polina, had a son in the army who was told, "If you dare even think you are leaving, you will be in prison too." Rosa's husband had eventually been released because his relatives in Moscow had paid a bribe, but both families were very frightened.

When the Consul came we asked him what to do and he advised lying low, and pretending they had given up the idea. As we had some time, Bagrat and I prayed and felt that we should go to Nagorno Karabakh and give the families this official advice. It would bring some encouragement in a difficult situation and we could also take them some provisions. It was arranged that we would travel by car with another man to drive us. So, with Vlasta, there would be four of us in the vehicle. Bagrat telephoned Rosa who was delighted with the idea and said she would put us up for the night. The journey would take around six to eight hours over three mountain passes – this was the plan.

The day before we were to set off, the weather suddenly changed for the worse. Heavy snow fell all night and the landscape in the morning was covered in a thick blanket of pristine white – beautiful but a portent of major transport problems! The temperature had also plummeted.

Everyone said, "Esther, you must not go." Common sense said the same thing. Bagrat, Vlasta, and I prayed. We all felt the Lord was saying, "Go!" Sometimes one has to act not on what can be seen and all the potential problems but rather on what the Lord is saying, as He can see all aspects of a situation while we can't.

Against our friends' advice, we set off, taking some food and a flask of coffee for the journey. We crossed the first range of mountains safely in bright sunshine. All was well until we came to the second set. As we began to wind our way up the incline, we saw lots of trucks and petrol tankers that had stopped at the side of the road; they seemed unable to proceed for some reason. We too stopped and our driver got out to see what the problem was. He returned saying something about ice but that gritting lorries were on their way, though no one knew exactly when they would arrive.

We backed down the slope and parked at the side of the road like the others; I began to pour out the coffee. At exactly this time an empty red dumper truck came past us, the driver making his way at good speed up the mountain and seemingly without trouble. Suddenly the vehicle stopped, lost its traction, and began to slide alarmingly backwards, out of control, zigzagging as it came careering down the mountain road.

Several things happened all at once and the reality of the danger we were in flashed before our minds in seconds, but there was little that could be done. The drivers of the dump truck abandoned ship as it came sliding downhill; we saw them jump out. Bagrat, seeing the truck coming straight for our vehicle, did the only sensible thing he could do in the seconds we had – he jumped out of our car. Our driver was already outside. I had just handed Vlasta a cup of coffee and was holding the flask – neither of us could act quickly enough and in any case didn't know how to open the car doors. Thoughts flashed through my mind that we would either be crushed or else the truck would push us over the side of the mountain. I shouted out loud, "Jesus, save us!" and what happened next was nothing but a miracle. The truck, which was sliding straight towards us, stopped a metre before it touched us. It then slid a little more at an angle and came to a full halt.

Vlasta and I stared at it, stunned and breathless. She was shaking, poor thing, and had splashed hot coffee over herself. Then suddenly a feeling of great wonder and peace filled the car and we knew it had been God's intervention that had saved our lives. Bagrat and our driver, plus some others, came running towards us to see what had happened and all were completely amazed at our escape – they had been expecting a disaster. I have no doubt that an angelic hand stopped that truck and just in time. We were in awe of what the Lord had done to save our lives.

After a little time of rest and prayer, we decided that if the truck had almost made it to the top of the hill it would probably be OK for us, a much lighter vehicle, to try too. We set off and prayed in tongues all the way. If we paused in our prayers, the car slowed down and juddered, but as long as we prayed, we made good progress and were soon at the top. How we praised God, singing continually as we drove along! We soon crossed the next mountain range and started going down the other side. We had left the other vehicles stuck at the side of the first incline, but our troubles were not over yet.

The road winding its way down this side of the mountain was not smooth but rather full of potholes. Many of these were filled with snow so that they appeared just like a normal road surface; others were filled with water. The little car bumped in and out of all these hazards until, like a donkey pushed beyond its endurance, its overworked little engine couldn't take any more and finally stopped.

Our driver got out, checked the engine, and returned shaking his head.

"It's no good; it won't go," he said.

We looked at each other and then prayed. "Try it again," we urged the driver.

His expression told us that we would really need a miracle, but dutifully he turned the key. Amazingly the engine roared into life.

"Hallelujah!" we cried, and off we went again.

In all, this happened three times. Each time, the driver told us that the engine wouldn't go any further, and each time we prayed it started up again. It was incredible. It was obvious that the spiritual enemy of our souls and of Israel did not want us going to Nagorno Karabakh to see these Jewish people. But God did, and we were on His mission and He was making sure we got through. What an awesome God we serve! If He hadn't answered our prayers and kept the car going, we would have been stuck in the freezing weather on that mountain for hours – maybe even all night. But our God reigns and He made sure we got through. In the book of Hebrews the Lord says:

Never will I leave you;
never will I forsake you.

(Hebrews 13:5 NIV)

We proved the truth of this promise.

Hours later than expected, we arrived in the main town of Stepanakert and stopped in the central square while the driver got out and inspected our vehicle. There was something broken over the right front wheel and we could drive the car no longer. How we managed to get to Stepanakert we didn't know, other than by the grace of God. He got us through.

Looking at a sketched version of the map, we realized that Rosa, the lady we had come to see, lived a little way down the hill from the square and so we pushed the car down the street to a warm welcome. And what a welcome it was, with many hugs and a lovely meal that Rosa had prepared. Polina came too, which enabled us to talk to everyone involved. They all agreed with what we said. Rosa's husband, a well-known composer, was an asset to his country, and his desire to leave and go to Israel had provoked anger in some quarters.

He was a big man but with tears in his eyes he begged me to get his children out.

"Please, please, Esther, do all you can," he pleaded.

His two children were also very talented musically and played for us on the violin and piano. They were highly skilled and I was moved by their father's plea. Bagrat and I determined to find a way to get them to Israel.

Our driver meanwhile had scoured the locality for the car part that we needed. It seemed impossible to find what he required and so we decided to go back by bus the next morning. The driver would then buy the part in Yerevan and return to Stepanakert by bus to fit the part and drive the car home.

Our journey back to Yerevan took from 8.00 a.m. until midnight because of the bad weather conditions. There had been a lot of snow and the low temperatures had caused the diesel in the bus to freeze. Burning newspaper under it helped it to thaw out and by doing this frequently we made our way slowly back over the mountains. It was a very weary group of travellers that were met by our faithful friends in Yerevan.

Our driver located the part he needed in town and, with another believer for company, set off on the bus back over the mountains to Stepanakert. These poor brothers were on the bus for twenty-five hours because the weather was so bad – spending all night in the cold. Then, to make matters worse, they found when they had fitted the part that the left-hand side was broken too; our driver hadn't noticed it before. This poor man was exhausted and thoroughly fed up. He did not want to face two more bus journeys to fetch yet another part so he prayed, "Lord, if You will start this car, I will trust You to keep it going safely over the mountains back to Yerevan, just as You brought us here." He did not tell the other brother but just turned the key in the ignition and started the car. He drove it all the way back over the rough road and three mountain ranges straight to the repair garage, all in eight hours.

The mechanic took one look at it and said, "How on earth have you driven this car? It's impossible to drive!"

We rejoiced when we heard the driver's testimony. With God, nothing is impossible.

The cold deepened, the days passed, and we waited for news of the flight. Eventually we were told that the plane would be coming the next week, which was the first week in December; which day, no one knew.

Vlasta had to go back, so we sadly said farewell to her and provisionally arranged for buses to pick up the olim when the day of the flight came. I packed my things too as I would be travelling with them to Israel. My visa was due to expire and I was told that I had to hand in my passport and it would take six days to process. This was too long. If I went more than two days past the date of expiry, I could be in serious trouble.

Still the plane did not come. We were told it would now arrive the following week. People started to get anxious as they had saved just enough food to last until the flight and now this had to be rationed out for an extra week.

Apart from that, the temperatures outside were dropping still further and the roads were covered in deep snow with ice underneath. Each day, we met at 10.00 a.m. in the hall in the centre of town; Villie would call us in and together we would wait for news. Each day it was the same: "The plane is coming tomorrow." We dared not unpack our luggage just in case the plane really did come and so we were wearing more or less the same clothes every day. In addition, the trip to the hall and back to the apartment was hazardous because of the snow and ice. A serious fall at this time could be problematic as the person might not be allowed to board the plane. Many of the Jewish people stayed indoors and sent one member of their family to the meeting; usually that person had to walk there and back. At least Ashot had a car and so we could ride.

Five days passed; then on the evening of the fifth day I was in Ashot's home when at 9.00 p.m. the phone rang. The plane had arrived and I was to come immediately to a hotel in the centre of Yerevan to arrange the transport for the olim. Outside we saw that thick fog had set in. There were no lights of course, so very carefully we made our way to the hotel where someone from the Jewish Agency (Mr "B") was waiting for us along with Villie and Sasha.

Mr B introduced himself and said we must immediately gather the olim because he had another appointment and no time to waste.

I was appalled. "How can we do that at this time of night?" I asked him. "It's thick fog out there and no bus drivers are going to go and collect people at this late hour." (It was now after 10.00 p.m.) "Besides," I continued, "we don't know where many of them are as they're staying with friends."

He argued a little, reiterating how pressurized he was, and then asked how many we could assemble.

"About forty," I answered.

"OK then," he said, "we'll just take those forty."

"Oh no you won't," I replied indignantly. "We'll wait until tomorrow and take them all. I'm not leaving any behind. They've waited all this time, sold their homes and belongings, and we are not going without them."

Mr B looked at me, shrugged, and then went to phone someone. He returned and told me I was causing him a lot of trouble but, yes, we could go in the morning. We returned to the apartment some time after midnight to get some sleep, thankful that at last we were on our way and that no one would be left behind.

We awoke the next morning to blue skies and sunshine – a thaw had set in. The buses went round collecting the olim, and it wasn't too long before we had 115 people assembled at the airport with their luggage. Of course none of them had changed their clothes much in the previous five days as their luggage had all been packed. *Oh what does it matter?* I thought. *In a few hours we'll all be in Israel.*

The Jewish Agency man, Mr B, together with Villie and Sasha, disappeared to arrange the check-in procedure while the rest of us waited. The morning passed and there was still no news. In fact there was no movement of any sort.

There were few proper seats so people were leaning on walls, and children were making the best use they could of the boxes and bags that were going to be checked in. Again it occurred to me how patient these people were, waiting and waiting without the comforts that Westerners enjoy during flight delays, such as lounges and cafés.

After some time, a message came that there were discussions going on regarding the route we would take. It transpired that we were first going to fly north to Sochi in Georgia where we would change planes; then we would fly with Sochi Airlines to Israel. This was because we were not allowed to fly over Iran carrying olim bound for Israel. Neither would Turkey allow a plane from its old enemy Armenia to fly over its airspace. A plane from Sochi, however, would be allowed to fly over Turkey. So that was the plan.

This threw up another problem. The airport authorities now said we had to go through International Departures when really a flight within the fSU, such as the one to Sochi, could have gone through the domestic departure hall. It turned out that by sending us through the international hall the authorities could charge us more money! Always it was the same – any excuse to make more money from us.

We collected our luggage and carried it all the way round the building to International Departures. Again we waited . . . and waited . . . and waited. By now the olim had eaten their supplies of food. Among those gathered were the elderly, babies, toddlers, older children, disabled people, two diabetics, and a child who twice a week needed dialysis. Thankfully his parents had timed his treatment with the flight in mind and there were two days to spare so we thought this should not be a problem.

We prayed and prayed about all these extra complications, and later in the evening we all had to walk back again to the other terminal. At about 9.00 p.m. the airport authorities started to check us in, taking a very long time with each family.

Suddenly I remembered my visa, now several days overdue. I prayed and put some dollars into my pocket, thinking that if I put them on the counter with my passport, the officer would ignore the date; this often worked apparently when people were in such a predicament. As I approached the counter, I distinctly heard the Holy Spirit say, "Put the dollars away," so I did as I was told.

When one is doing God's business, He takes care of everything and knows exactly what will happen in any given situation. I handed in my passport a little nervously and watched the official open it. Inside was a blank piece of paper with just a date on it and nothing else; I had received this on arriving in Armenia. He lifted it out, smiled, and then stamped my passport and the paper, handing both back to me and then waving me through. I was amazed! He either had not noticed my out-of-date visa or else had chosen to ignore it.

By about midnight we had all passed through check-in and were waiting to board the plane. Everyone was very tired but at last we could get on the plane and sit down, which was such a relief. We were given drinks of water, and at about 2.00 a.m. we taxied out to the runway and took off, landing in Sochi about an hour later.

The entire cargo was unloaded and put in a heap; there were no carousels. Each person had to find his or her own luggage despite being exhausted, and yet these dear sweet people did not complain. It took quite a while for each family to separate their own cases and boxes, but finally it was completed.

Outside there were buses to take us to a hotel, where it transpired we had to wait until later in the day for our flight to Israel. Not too bad, one might think; but first we had to be checked *out*. There seemed no end to the unnecessary bureaucracy in these former Soviet countries.

When it was my turn I suddenly realized that I did not have a Russian visa to enter Georgia as is required. Again I fingered the dollars in my pocket and again I heard the Holy Spirit say "No" as I handed over my passport. The officer looked inside, took out the mysterious piece of paper, stamped it, put it back, and smiled at me as he handed everything back without a question. He did not even stamp the passport itself. *What did he think the piece of paper was?* I wondered.

It was pouring with rain as everyone walked to the buses, each family carrying their own luggage but helping one another as best they could. Soon we were driving through Sochi towards our hotel and suddenly people noticed that the streets were lit. "*Svet! Svet!*" (Light! Light!), they called out excitedly. It was such a joy for these Jewish people to see the street lights! People in the West have no idea what it's like to live for months on end in semi-darkness, with only candles for light, while sitting in freezing temperatures.

At the hotel, for some reason the bus driver parked in a space some way from the entrance, and everyone had to carry the luggage up to the hotel foyer and stack it there. I just don't know how these people managed, for each of them had about 60 kilograms.

Once inside, we found that the hotel was not expecting us and so were not prepared. *What else can go wrong?* I thought. The night porter, not happy at being woken at 4.30 a.m., took some time to find a member of staff to check us in. This again was a painfully slow process. No beds had been made, there was no heating on, and there was no hot water. It took ages to sort it all out. The elderly, those with special needs, and those with children were given rooms first.

Because all the luggage had to be kept in the foyer, two stalwart old ladies decided that they would not go to bed but would sit up all night and guard it. I had come across this attitude before with people from the fSU – they trusted no one. As far as they were concerned, nothing was safe.

I enquired about breakfast and was told this would be at 9.00 a.m. so dutifully passed the message on to everyone else. Finally I got to my small, unheated room, a bed with no blankets or sheets, and only cold water. *Never mind*, I thought, *I'm used to cold water for washing.* As I had no means of changing clothes, I lay down for a prayer and some sleep.

At 8.45 a.m. I went out to find breakfast. As if things couldn't get any worse, I discovered there wasn't any! I asked to see someone in authority and was taken to the office of a stern-looking woman who spoke good English. She informed me that the Jewish Agency hadn't given them any money for food because all arrangements with the hotel had for some reason been cancelled; this was the reason there was no food.

I pleaded with her, telling her that the people had had no proper meal now for twenty-four hours and there were children, babies, elderly people, and diabetics.

"You cannot do this to them," I said firmly.

She was adamant that without money she would not provide food; that was that. There would be no breakfast, no lunch, nothing. I was stunned. In fact I was heartbroken at her callousness. How could anyone do this to these hungry people?

I threw a quick "Help me" prayer heavenward, and found myself asking how much money would cover the food. A thought came into my mind that I had some English money in my luggage that was to cover my flight home from Israel. It was £160. *Will it be enough?* I wondered.

The cost of the breakfast in roubles was calculated for all of us, and then the cost for lunch. I fetched my English currency from my room and handed it to the hotel manager. I estimated that it would be enough but the woman would probably need to check with the bank. She held up the notes to the light as if intimating I might have just printed them; she had never seen sterling notes before and was inquisitive. Then she picked up the phone and had a conversation with somebody at the bank; I could tell she was explaining the cost of the food in roubles and the amount of English currency I had. She put the phone down and I held my breath.

"Yes," she said, "this will cover all the food."

Oh the relief! God is so marvellous. He had answered again. I had quite forgotten that I had this money.

I asked her how long it would be to breakfast.

"About forty minutes," she answered.

I passed the word to everyone else but in the end it took a little longer than estimated. Never mind, there was food and that was what mattered – sausages, reconstituted egg, bread, and tea. The olim crowded into the dining room and when they had finished eating there was not one crumb left; they had been absolutely famished.

The family with the child needing dialysis had gone off to the local hospital, but others put some food aside for them. After everyone had eaten they all went back to bed to rest.

In the middle of the afternoon, lunch was served and again the olim crowded into the dining room to enjoy their meal. Somehow word had got round that I had paid for the food. I tried to assure them that it was God who had organized it, but they were very grateful to me nonetheless.

The family that had gone to the hospital returned in time for their lunch, but before they could finish it word came that buses were outside to take us all to the airport.

Before we left, the stern-faced director called me into her office and handed back my passport. In it was all the English currency that I had used to pay for the food. I just looked at her and she said, "I'm afraid there was a mistake. The money for food had in fact been paid but no one had told me."

I wondered what the truth really was. Still, God had worked it all out. He had prompted me to pay and then given me back the money for my ticket to England. Hallelujah! He never fails to amaze me.

Soon we were on the buses and off to the airport once more. We were there by 5.00 p.m. and waited in the departure hall. Once more we waited and waited. As in Yerevan airport there were few seats and the time seemed to pass slowly. Eventually people arrived and we assumed check-in would begin. But no – these were the cleaners! We had to watch them mop the hall right through, using buckets of dirty water, which they slopped everywhere and then mopped up again. Then we waited until the floors were dry. We had been in the hall almost four hours and nothing had happened.

At 9.00 p.m. check-in staff arrived and thankfully the process began, albeit slowly. Each person had to have their luggage checked and then present their passport. The officials were somewhat less fussy with my luggage, perhaps because I was British.

When I was called forward to present my passport I again remembered I had no visa and wondered what would be said this time. As before, the officer took the piece of paper out, stamped it, and this time kept it. He handed me back my passport without any questions.

I had entered the fSU without a visa and now was leaving without a visa. To this day I wonder what they thought the piece of paper was. Did God cause them to think it was a visa? I don't know. All I did know was that with God nothing is impossible.

After each person's luggage had been checked and passport inspected, we had to go through a doorway where a very fat, severe-looking woman scowled at us. Her purpose in sitting there scowling remained a mystery but, as I had found out, in the fSU such mysteries were not uncommon and one just had to accept them without fuss.

Once past her, we were in the departure lounge with the luxury of somewhere to sit! Encouragingly we could see our plane from here, and as the luggage was checked and started to stack up we began to relax. Not for long, though.

Villie came rushing through to me. "Esther, there is one family they're not allowing to come through. Something isn't right with the mother's papers."

"What?" I exclaimed. "Go back and insist they let them come!"

He disappeared, but soon returned shaking his head.

"It's no good," he said. "They will not let her come. The husband and child can come but not her."

"Villie, go back and insist," I pressured.

"Esther, you don't understand; these are Russians – they never give in."

Poor Villie was really rattled by these officials, so I went back to reason with them myself.

The family was standing there, looking very pale with tears running down their cheeks. I spoke with the official behind the desk, explaining that these people were Armenians with authority to leave Armenia and authority to enter Israel. They were not Russians and he had no business stopping them going on the flight.

It was no use. He thumped the counter and said, "We are in charge here. They are *not* going."

I made my way back past the scowling woman, whose expression had strangely changed to one of triumph. I could see the huge pile of luggage stacked up and the three dear ones being left behind.

In the departure lounge everyone was disheartened. I could imagine what they were thinking: *Will we ever go?*

I began to pray, walking up and down, and regardless of what anyone thought I shouted out to God: "Lord, Your Word says, 'I will gather them . . . leaving none behind.' You, Lord, are calling these people home to Israel; they are obeying You. You said, 'Let My people go.' We tell you, Satan, take your hands off! Let these people go. You have *no* right trying to keep any here. Not one shall be left behind!"

The people sat up, watching me. Suddenly the door opened and the family came through, looking bewildered and shaken. They did not know what had happened. Suddenly the officer had said, "Oh go – get out of here!" and so they did, quickly!

Thinking about it afterwards, I wondered if God had made the officials unwilling to search through the mountain of luggage for this family's bags and boxes because it was late and time to go home from work. Whatever the reason, God had changed their minds and put it in their hearts to let this family go. Praise the Lord!

Almost as one voice, the olim started saying, "This is our God, this is our God! Esther prayed and God did it! This is our God."

It had often been the case that as we brought Jewish people out of the fSU, problems ensued which required prayer. As God answered these prayers He would prove His faithfulness to the olim and they would see it for themselves. They knew we were Christians and it was a great witness to them. Hallelujah!

At last we were free to board the plane. It was bliss to sit down, drink a glass of juice, be served a meal by lovely stewardesses, and be treated like royalty. It was about 1.30 a.m. as we took off. Everyone was soon asleep, exhausted from the rigours of what they'd been through.

We arrived in Ben Gurion airport at about 3.00 a.m. What a joy it was to come down the steps of the plane and be greeted by that special scent that seems to shout, "You're in Israel!" Most of us were in tears, hugging one another. Some even knelt to kiss the ground – home at last.

A strange feeling filled my heart as if I myself were fulfilling my destiny. It seemed like a dream. Suddenly I saw Gustav and he'd brought with him a friend, Ted Walker. They had been at the airport three nights running to see if we would arrive. What joy filled my heart to see them! There were more hugs and tears.

Once inside the terminal, we were permitted to go into the Absorption Hall and had the privilege of witnessing the olim being welcomed into Israel. The children were given a bag of sweets and an Israeli flag. The adults were able to phone home to relatives to say they had arrived safely, and there was food and drink if anyone should need it.

Each family was interviewed and everything arranged to help them settle – even tickets for taxis to their destinations. It was very impressive. With hugs and tears we said our farewells.

Ted Walker drove us to Gustav's flat in Jerusalem where Elsa was waiting for us. Gustav admitted that we had all looked like a group of vagabonds: unkempt and the men unshaven. I wasn't surprised. He ran a very deep bath laced with Elsa's bath oils and sent me to have a good soak. Oh, it was like heaven, after so many weeks of spartan living, to lie right under the water and to get really clean – marvellous! Elsa washed all my clothes in her machine and dried them for me. I slept and slept.

What a journey it had been – two days and nights instead of one and a half hours. How Satan had tried his best to stop us! But God had prevailed. The way to Israel had been truly blasted open, and Jewish people have been returning from Armenia ever since.

CHAPTER 9

HOW THE INGATHERING FROM ARMENIA CONTINUES

When I have brought them back from the nations and have gathered them from the countries of their enemies, I will be proved holy through them in the sight of many nations. Then they will know that I am the LORD their God, for though I sent them into exile among the nations, I will gather them to their own land, not leaving any behind.

(Ezekiel 39:27–28 TNIV)

The third flight from Armenia, which was paid for by Gustav Scheller, took place in November 1994. The following spring, his ship the *Dmitry Shostakovich* started the trip again across the Black Sea to Haifa from the Ukrainian port of Odessa. This was the way God had shown him to take olim to Israel, allowing them to take many more of their personal belongings than if they had flown. People were even able to take pets; the crowning glory was one family's beloved horse which successfully made the three-day crossing.

Gustav thought it would be a good idea if, instead of taking direct flights to Israel, olim flew from Yerevan in Armenia to the port of Odessa and then joined the ship for the sea crossing to Haifa. It would be much less expensive. There was another advantage in that there would be less hassle over the flights because Yerevan-to-Odessa would be considered a domestic trip as both cities were within the fSU. I therefore set off once again for Armenia, complete with boxes of much-needed aid.

Things were a great deal easier this time in that the Jewish people trusted us and needed no persuasion to make aliyah – they were ready to go. Their leaders were willing to help too, as were the church leaders. We had broken through all the efforts of the Enemy to interfere with the flights and we praised God for His enabling power and for those who faithfully backed us in prayer.

For the first trip, twenty-four olim were gathered. We didn't consider this number as being too low as we knew we could send a group each month. These olim were not able to take as much luggage as the folk in Odessa who were not catching a flight. They were allowed 250 kg of luggage each. Our olim from Armenia were limited to 45 kg, a huge difference. To help this situation, dear Gustav made an extra payment so that each person getting the flight from Armenia was allowed 64 kg. It was a wonderful gesture.

To my great amazement and joy, the one couple from Kirovaken who had remained behind on the earlier flight were now among those gathered. God had seen to it. The husband, who was at first reluctant to leave because of his job, had been made redundant. News had come from their relatives in Israel about how good life was there and the family was now eager to join them. The Lord has His ways!

The flight from Yerevan went without problems except for one. A young man from Bagrat's group had been assigned to come with me to learn about the work. Such young men were usually stopped by the airport authorities as they were needed in the army. Sure enough, as we went to board the plane I saw this lad surrounded by armed militia. He looked really scared. Suddenly out of my mouth came the words in English: "Hey, what are you doing? He's my interpreter!" Amazingly the militia just stepped aside and let him go. Yet again God had intervened.

After a relatively short flight we landed in Odessa and went to collect our luggage. The airport there was small and there was no carousel; the luggage was just put in a heap and passengers had to find their own. Once everyone had claimed their bags and gone through to the arrivals area, we found help waiting in the form of volunteers from Operation Exodus. Strong young men helped carry the luggage, and a couple of pretty girls were there to assist the children. The look on the faces of our olim said it all: they were amazed – these poor people who had always felt so hated by others.

At the Operation Exodus base the olim were given accommodation for a couple of nights. The evening before sailing, everyone was summoned to a meeting to be given last-minute instructions. There was much to be done, especially down at the port with the Ukrainian customs officers, and the olim needed to know what was going to happen to them, otherwise it could be a stressful time. At the end of all the instructions, musicians and singers entertained the olim with Hebrew songs, and one could feel the atmosphere becoming more relaxed.

The next morning, buses took everyone down to the port. It was a sombre place, overlooked by the infamous Potemkin Steps, a long flight of steps leading from the top of a hill down to the harbour. Here, during the Second World War, some Jews had tried to flee captivity but soldiers were waiting on these steps and had gunned them down. Ukraine had seen many such atrocities. In fact many Christians felt that something in the demonic realm had been strengthened because of all the innocent blood spilt, and had called in a group called Ellel Ministries from the UK to assist with praying into this problem. Little did I know at that time that the Lord would later lead me into an involvement with this ministry, which proved to be a great blessing.

Once the ship was under way, everyone started to relax and enjoy themselves. The olim had never seen such food as they enjoyed onboard ship. Their faces were a picture. There was time to rest, read, and chat; to renew acquaintances and to make new friends. It was a very blessed time.

The ship took three days to make the journey across the Black

Sea, through the Bosphorus and Sea of Marmara and down the coast of Turkey to Haifa. When the ship passed through Istanbul, people were out on deck gazing at sights they had never seen – a new land. We were so near we could see the people busying themselves along the waterfront, and there were many ships making their way in both directions through this narrow strip of water that separated the two continents of Europe and Asia.

All this new-found wonder was nothing compared to the excitement on deck as we neared Haifa and the olim caught sight of the Promised Land for the first time. They lined the railings on the top deck, some very emotional as the dream of Jewish hearts for two millennia got visibly nearer and nearer, finally becoming a reality as we pulled into the harbour.

As we came off the ship, volunteers pushed trolleys laden with our luggage. I helped a lady who was visibly distressed about her belongings. No doubt at some time in the past she had had a bad experience that made her worry about her possessions. She seemed sure that her things would be stolen.

"*Nash vieshi! Nash vieshi!*" (Our things! Our things!) she kept shouting, running her hands through her hair and making it stand up on end. Aware as I was of her distress, there was nothing I could do in the middle of the crowd of passengers to reassure her.

Then in a few minutes, at the top of a ramp, her luggage reappeared, and her mood changed. She was amazed. She flung her arms around my neck, kissing me profusely and covering me with bright red lipstick.

"*Eta Israel, nash Israel!*" (It's Israel, our Israel!) she shouted in Russian. That said it all. These people might have had bad experiences in the fSU and have suffered much abuse, but ahead lay a new life in the Holy Land!

Once all the olim had gone through immigration and been met by the Ministry of Absorption, our job was done. I stayed on in Haifa for a few days together with Karine, one of Ashot's sisters who had been a volunteer on the ship.

One morning we went into the city centre to look around and decided to buy a cup of coffee. We both felt impressed to sit outside at a certain table. We had hardly sat down when we heard a child's voice shouting, "Karine, Karine!" It was a young girl who had come to Israel on a previous sailing and had recognized Karine. Behind her was her father, and he and Karine were soon in conversation in Russian. He invited us to see his apartment as it was so much better than the place he'd had in the fSU.

He led the way to the block where he lived. We were about to enter the front door when someone called me from upstairs. I turned and looked up the stairwell, and couldn't believe my eyes. It was the lady from Yerevan who had had such a struggle with the Consul to convince him that she was Jewish. Because I had intervened, he had agreed to have the archives searched in the town of Baku. And it had obviously yielded fruit, for here she was! I couldn't believe it – what a coincidence! The lady was so happy. She had all eight members of her family with her and they were really settling in well. She didn't even have to work to supplement the family's income but could spend her days relaxing in the sunshine and playing with her grandchildren. Meeting her was such a gift from the Lord. We cried in each other's arms. God had answered our prayers and she was here in the Land. We have such a faithful God.

This trip was the first of many bringing Jews from Armenia via Odessa; they continued until Operation Exodus ceased using the ship and started connecting with flights run by the Jewish Agency.

Armenian olim now make their way to Tbilisi in Georgia and fly from there direct to Israel along with Georgian olim. I continued working with the Armenian groups for two more flights and then handed the whole project over to Bagrat and his team. Since then a young man called Arsen has taken it over.

Jews are still being found in Armenia, though fewer and fewer as the years pass. Surely soon they will all be in Israel. We were originally told there were about 300 but since then more than 1,000 have made aliyah. The mathematics goes something like this: $300 - 164 = 478 - 250 = 623$ and so on. In other words there are really more Jews there than people think! They come out to admit their Jewish identity when they feel it is safe to do so. May they all come, as the Scripture says, "not leaving any behind" (Ezekiel 39:27–28 TNIV).

> But now, thus says the LORD, your creator, O Jacob,
> And He who formed you, O Israel,
> "Do not fear, for I have redeemed you;
> I have called you by name; you are Mine!
> "When you pass through the waters, I will be with you;
> And through the rivers, they will not overflow you.
> When you walk through the fire, you will not be scorched,
> Nor will the flame burn you . . .
> "Do not fear, for I am with you;
> I will bring your offspring from the east,
> And gather you from the west.
> "I will say to the north, 'Give them up!'
> And to the south, 'Do not hold them back.'
> Bring My sons from afar,
> And My daughters from the ends of the earth . . .
> "Even from eternity I am He;
> And there is none who can deliver out of My hand;
> I act and who can reverse it?"
>
> (Isaiah 43:1–2, 5–6, 13)

Epilogue

Once the work in Armenia had been taken over by the local believers, I returned to England. It was not long before Hannah told me of her recent visit to Khabarovsk in the far east of Russia, taking Christian literature. She told me how a friend of hers had been on the Kamchatka Peninsula. This was about as far east as one could go in the fSU, and the area had been off limits to Westerners until then.

A little "bell" rang in my head – I had a contact there. In fact I had had the name and address for about seven years. Back in 1989 when visiting a church in Kiev to which I had given some Bibles, a short, stocky lady had given me a slip of paper. Written on it in Russian was a request to me to bring Bibles to a village called Korf on the Kamchatka Peninsula. At the time, I had no idea how I would get there so had just filed the piece of paper somewhere. The Lord was now nudging me to get it out! It was time to go and fulfil the request to take Bibles to this lady.

The journey was the first of many more adventures finding Jewish people in the most unlikely places . . .

The Lord has clearly outlined His purpose for Israel in His Word –
the Bible. Israel and the Jewish people are to be a testimony to God's
existence, His character, and His faithfulness. Israel proves that His
Word is true.

> *Let all the earth fear the LORD;*
> *Let all the inhabitants of the world stand in awe of Him.*
> *For He spoke and it was done;*
> *He commanded, and it stood fast.*
> *The LORD nullifies the counsel of the nations;*
> *He frustrates the plans of the peoples.*
> *The counsel of the LORD stands forever,*
> *The plans of His heart from generation to generation.*
>
> (Psalm 33:8–11)

ABOUT THE AUTHORS

ESTHER LEVER

Esther Lever became a Christian as a child around 1946. She knew nothing about Israel or the Jewish people until the Lord called her to go to Israel following the death of her husband in 1982. It was while volunteering in the Land that she saw the prophecies of the Word of God being fulfilled before her eyes. She learned about the re-establishment of the State in 1948 and witnessed the ingathering of the people from many lands.

Drawn by the Lord, Esther visited the former Soviet Union many times before becoming involved in helping the Jewish people to return to Israel through working with Ebenezer Operation Exodus. Later this resulted in her travelling all over the world seeking out Jewish people, encouraging them from the Word of God, and helping them to emigrate to Israel, or "make *aliyah*."

Having a wide knowledge of prophetic Scripture, she has taught in churches and fellowships in many places about the purposes of God for Israel. She encourages congregations to establish prayer groups and to support the work of assisting the Jewish people to return to the "Promised Land."

Esther continues to travel abroad several times a year and

is currently the Thames Regional Representative for Ebenezer Operation Exodus.

You may contact the author about this book by writing to estherlever80@gmail.com

RUSSELL BOWLES

Russell Bowles became a Christian in 1975 and almost from the beginning became aware that there was something special and prophetic about the Jewish people. The following year he went on a young people's tour to Israel and was profoundly impacted by what he saw and the people he met. A lifelong interest in Israel followed.

Russell works as a freelance writer and speaker, and lives in Merseyside with his wife and family.

We hope you enjoyed reading this
Sovereign World book.
For more details of other Sovereign
books and new releases see our website:

www.sovereignworld.com

Find us on Twitter @sovereignworld

Our authors welcome your feedback on their books.
Please send your comments to our offices at. You can request
to subscribe to our email and mailing list online or by writing to:

**Sovereign World Ltd, PO Box 784,
Ellel, Lancaster, LA1 9DA, United Kingdom
info@sovereignworld.com**

Sovereign World titles are available from
all good Christian bookshops and eBook vendors.
For information about our distributors in the UK, USA, Canada,
South Africa, Australia and Singapore, visit:
www.sovereignworld.com/trade

If you would like to help us send a copy of this book and
many other titles to needy pastors in developing countries,
please write for further information or send your gift to:

Sovereign World Trust, PO Box 777,
Tonbridge, Kent TN11 0ZS
United Kingdom
www.sovereignworldtrust.org.uk

The Sovereign World Trust is a registered charity